You Be
the Judge

Also available in the Wiley Legal and Practical Guide Series:

*The Complete Guide to Buying,
Owning and Selling a Home in Canada*
by Margaret Kerr and JoAnn Kurtz

You Be the Judge

The Complete Canadian Guide to Resolving Legal Disputes Out of Court

Norman A. Ross

JOHN WILEY & SONS CANADA, LTD

Toronto · New York · Chichester · Weinheim · Brisbane · Singapore

John Wiley & Sons Canada, Ltd
22 Worcester Road
Etobicoke, Ontario
M9W 1L1

Canadian Cataloguing in Publication Data

Ross, Norman A., 1943–
    You be the judge : the complete Canadian guide to
resolving legal disputes out of court

Includes bibliographical references and index.
ISBN 0-471-64199-5

1. Dispute resolution (Law) – Canada – Popular works.
I. Title.

KE8615.R68 1997   347.71'09   C97-931496-8
KF9084.R68 1997

Production Credits
Cover concept: Christine Rae
Cover design: JAQ
Text design: Christine Rae
Printer: Tri-Graphic Printing Ltd.
Illustrator: Sue Scott

Printed in Canada
10 9 8 7 6 5 4 3 2 1

For my sister Toni

CONTENTS

Preface   xiii
Acknowledgements   xvii
Introduction   xxi

Chapter 1 Negotiation   1
  What You Need To Know About Negotiation Style   4
  Positional or Win/Lose Negotiation   5
  Deadlock   6
  The Deadly Circle   7
    Win/Lose Negotiation Produces Anger   7
    Vested Interests in Negotiation—The Zero-Sum Game   8
    Dammit, I'm Right And They're Wrong   8
  Bias and Subjective Evaluation   10
  Interest-Based or Win/Win Negotiation   11
  Best-Case Scenario or Walk-Away Position   11
  A Typical Interest-Based Negotiation   12
  What Style of Negotiation Best Suits Mediation?   13
  Reactive Devaluation   13
  Impasse in Negotiation   14
    The Whack-Um Game   14
    Diagnosing the Problem   14
    Additional Strategies to Break Impasse   15
  Litigation Mode is not Negotiation   16
  Power in Negotiation   18
    Power Imbalances   18
  Negotiating Tips   19
    Leave Them Better Than You Found Them   19
    Be Assertive, Not Rude   19
    Don't Complain or Explain   19
    Send Reinforcing Positive Messages   20
    Negotiate in Good Faith   20
    End the Negotiation On a Positive Note   20

Chapter 2 What is ADR?   **21**
   The Need For Change   21
   The Litigation Process   22
      Step 1   22
      Step 2   23
      Step 3   23
      Step 3A   23
      Step 4   23
      Step 5   23
      Step 6   23
      Step 7   24
      Step 8   24
      Step 9   24
      Step 10   24
      Step 11   24
   The Delay Factor   28
   The Historical Context   28
   ADR Street   29
      Negotiation   29
      Mediation   29
      The Mini-Mall   30
      Arbitration   31
      Rights-Based "Mediation"   31
      Court   32
   Mediation in Detail   32
   Advantages Of Mediation   33
   The Decision to Mediate   35
   Getting the Other Side to the Table   35
      Direct Approach   35
      Indirect Approach   36
      Government Mandates   36
      Other Inducements   36
   Should I Mediate?—Essential Elements   36
      Intent to Negotiate in Good Faith   36
      Authority   37
      Relationships—Is the Relationship Worth Preserving?   37
      Flexibility   37
   When is the Best Time to Mediate?   38
      The Role of the Lawyer   38
      The Stages of Litigation   39
      Possible Outcome of Trial and its Influence on Mediation 41
   When to Avoid Mediation   42
      Withheld Information   43
      The Single-Issue Dispute: All or Nothing   43
   Arbitration—An Alternative or Supplement to Mediation   44
      What is Arbitration?   45

Mediation vs. Arbitration   45
Mediation/Arbitration (Med-Arb)   45
   An Alternative   46

Chapter 3 The Mediation Process—A Step-by-Step Look at a Typical
     Mediation   49
Stage One—The Convening Stage   50
   The Agreement to Mediate   50
   Location   51
   How Long Should the Mediation Last?   51
Stage Two—Introductions and Ground Rules   52
   Intention   53
   Authority   53
   Goals   54
   Participation   55
Stage Three—Information Exchange and Issue Identification   55
   Watch, Listen, and Learn   55
   Opening Statements: You Are Up   56
   Opening Statements: They Are Up   57
   Clarification and Amplification   57
   The Break   58
Regrouping—What's Really Going On?   58
Private Meetings: Party-Mediator   58
   Process Options After the Break: Remain Separated or Resume
     Joint Session?   60
Reconvening   60
Remaining Separate to Develop Common Ground   61
Stage Four—Problem Solving   61
   Generating Options   62
   Testing Alternatives Against Your Walk-Away Position   62
   The Analysis   63
Valuable Non-Monetary Elements of Resolution   64
   Vindication/Saving Face   65
   Apology   66
   Money Now vs. Money Later   66
   Stress Avoidance   67
   Risk Aversion or Certainty   67
   Business Concessions   67
   Avoiding Bad Publicity   67
   Cost Avoidance   68
   Good Publicity   68
   Avoiding a Bad Precedent   68
Stage Five—Resolution   69
If Agreement isn't Possible   69
Mediation Process Checklist   72

Chapter 4 The Role of Mediators and Lawyers   **75**
  Mandatory Court–Connected Mediation   76
  Role of the Mediator   77
  Qualities of a Good Mediator   77
    History   78
    Experience and Training   78
  Must the Mediator Have Knowledge of the Issues?   79
  Does the Mediator Have to Have Insurance?   80
  Style of the Mediator   80
    Directive Mediation   80
    Interest-Based Mediation   81
  Mediator Ethics   82
    Coercion   82
    Mediators Must Not Provide Legal Advice or an Opinion   82
    Impartiality   82
    Conflict of Interest   82
    Mediator Must Respect Confidences   82
    Integrity of the Process   83
  How to Find the Right Mediator   83
    Buyer Beware   83
    Mediation Service Providers   84
    Mediator Associations   84
    Court Rosters   85
    Referral Service   85
  Role of the Lawyer   86
  Legal Ethics in Mediation   87
  Interview Guide Checklist   89

Chapter 5 Barriers to Success   **91**
  Anger   91
    How to Recognize Anger in Yourself and Others   93
    What to Do about Your Own Anger   94
    What to Do when Confronted by an Angry Opponent   95
    Anger and Mediation   95
    The Myth of Litigation   96
  Bottom Lines   96
    Heck, It Really is Only about Money   97
  Lack of Preparation   98
    Understand Your Interests   99
    Understand Their Interests   99
    Who Should Attend the Mediation?   99
    Consider Power, Cultural Differences, and Gender   100
    Anticipate Impasse or Deadlock   100
    Prepare a Mediation Brief   100
    The Law—It is Important   100
    Role at the Table   101
  Preparation Checklist   101

Disclosure of Information   102
    Getting Critical Information without Discoveries   102
    Your Information   103
    Their Information   103
Difficult People   103
Difficult Behaviour   104
Bad Timing   105
Unrealistic Expectations   106
Missing Party   107
Overemphasis on Settlement   108
Cultural Barriers   108
Power Imbalances   109
Lack of Resources   110
Institutional Barriers   111
What if the Mediation Becomes Deadlocked?   111

Chapter 6 Agreement   **113**
Getting There   113
Closure   113
Separate Proposals or Offers   114
Single-Text Agreement   114
Who Makes the First Move?   114
Momentum   114
Settlement Remorse   115
Hallmarks of a Good Agreement   115
Testing the Agreement   115
    Efficient   115
    Fair   116
    Durable   116
    Enforceable   116
The Agreement—Tips for Getting a Good Agreement   117
    Write it Up   117
    The Agreement is Public Unless Otherwise Stated   117
    If You Want it to Be Confidential, Say So   117
    Remember it is the *Parties'* Agreement   118
    Tie Down all Loose Ends   118
    Use the Mediator   118
    Don't Use the Mediator to Draft the Agreement   118
    Use a Dispute Resolution Clause   119
    Does the Agreement End the Dispute?   120
When it's Over, it's Over!   120
What Happens if the Agreement is Broken?   120
Non-Agreement   121

Chapter 7 All Disputes are Not the Same   **123**
Commercial Cases   124

Process Design   124
Personal Injury Claims   127
    Attitudes Towards Mediation   128
Disability Claims   131
Divorce and Family Mediation   132
Employment Disputes   135
    Emotions   136
    Preparation   137
    The Agreement to Resolve   137
Family Business Disputes   139
    Family Councils—Preventative Medicine   139
Construction Cases   140
    Construction Liens   141
    Partnering   141
Estate Disputes   143
    Estate Planning—Preventing Disputes   143
    Estate Disputes   144
Bankruptcy and Insolvency   146
    Timeliness   146
    Complexity   146
    Flexibility   146
    Problem Solving and Consensus Building   146
    Choice of Mediator   147
    Process   147
    Emotion   147
    Court Supervision Not Dismissed   147
Multiparty/Multiissue Disputes   149
    Mediator's Knowledge of the Issues   150
Medical Malpractice   150
    Timing of the Mediation   151
    Appropriate Party   152
    Complaints about Doctors and Other Health-Care Professionals   152
Government Disputes   154
Neighbourhood and Community Disputes   156

Chapter 8 Conclusion   159

Appendix A   163
Glossary of Dispute Resolution Terms   163

Appendix B   173
Agreement to Mediate   173

Appendix C   177
Arbitration and Mediation Institute of Canada Inc. Code of Ethics   177
Model Standards of Conduct for Mediators   178

List of References   185

Index   189

PREFACE

In everyday life you are often faced with situations which require you or someone else to intervene to resolve a disagreement:

- Your two friends are not speaking and you meet with them to try to resolve their differences.
- You intervene when your parents have a spat.
- You are at odds with a co-worker and your boss meets with the two of you to see if things can be worked out.
- Your children are fighting in the back seat of your car.
- Your cats are fighting over a new toy. (Well, sometimes it's best to leave well enough alone.)

Almost everyday you are either a mediator (someone who is neutral and intervenes to obtain resolution or reconciliation) or a disputing party in need of a mediator. And you know that mediation often works on a personal level day to day.

But what about disputes that are not personal, but legal or business-related?

Anyone who has ever been involved in a lawsuit can attest to how long, slow, inefficient, frustrating, and expensive a process a lawsuit can be. A new alternative to resolving civil cases is mediation, or Alternative Dispute Resolution (ADR). Much as with personal disputes, a neutral third party meets with the disputing parties and helps them to negotiate a settlement on terms which they not only find acceptable but create for themselves. Instead of a long, costly court battle in which a judge decides who wins and loses, mediation takes place earlier in the process of litigation, usually costs a great deal less than litigation, and often results in a win-win resolution in which all parties feel some degree of satisfaction. ADR helps to preserve relationships, reduce emotional strain and frustration, and reduce legal fees.

The Ontario government has shown leadership by announcing in January 1997 that starting with the Toronto region and thereafter throughout the province over the following four years, all civil cases other than family and construction cases will be required to mediate before being permitted to continue the lawsuit unless exempted by a court official.

The objective of this book is to assist all Canadians, whether they are business people or individuals embroiled in disputes, to better understand and utilize mediation and other ADR processes. Whether the dispute involves an insurance claim, a claim for worker's or other compensation, family inheritance, a commercial problem, or divorce, this book can help. It is designed to:

- demystify and simplify mediation and other ADR processes;
- put you in charge of your dispute;
- help you ask your lawyer and other advisors informed questions and let you decide whether ADR is suitable for you;
- assist you to select the appropriate mediation team;
- help you to prepare yourself and your team thoroughly for successful mediation;
- take you through a step-by-step review of what will happen so there will be no surprises;
- anticipate many of the problems that might be encountered and provide the means to successfully overcome them.

I chose the title *You Be the Judge* because the central theme of the book is that in mediation, you—no one else, not your lawyer, the mediator, or your opponent—are in control from beginning to end.

The book is not a training aid per se and certainly is no substitute for the skills that mediation experience builds. However, the book is intended to provide readers with the kinds of details they would learn if they were able to take mediation training.

You Be the Judge is written primarily for people who wish to use mediation as an alternative to litigation. This audience includes business and professional people, such as insurance adjusters, corporate counsel, property development, and financial industry executives; individuals who have been injured in the workplace, an auto collision, a fall; people involved in divorce proceedings, failed business transactions, real estate deals, or disputes concerning inheritance; as well as their lawyers and other advisors. The book is also intended for anyone involved in a quarrel or misunderstanding that threatens to balloon into a lawsuit.

The book is also written for lawyers who have no desire to become mediators but who do have a substantial interest in ensuring that both they and their clients are effective and well prepared permitting all parties to attain the maximum benefits of this new and exciting process. The book provides a practical approach to understanding and using the principles and techniques necessary to accomplish this.

The book begins by explaining ADR and the various types of ADR commonly available and how they fit into the overall context of negotiation, the key building block of ADR. The chapter examines negotiation pragmatically and explains how to identify and apply principled negotiation to any dispute being prepared for mediation. The next chapter's topics include the advantages of mediation, optimal timing, some good reasons to avoid mediation, and a discussion of the available alternatives.

Chapter 3, The Mediation Process, begins with a discussion of an agreement to mediate followed by a detailed step-by-step analysis of a mediation from beginning to end, with tips on how to maximize the process. The process is reviewed from various perspectives including that of the mediator so as to remove any mystery or apprehension which might be present if the mediator's point of view is not clearly understood. Examples are used to illustrate how mediation can provide wider, richer outcomes than are possible in litigation.

Chapter 4 focuses on the roles of the mediator and lawyer and how to choose the right one. It includes details of the kinds of questions to ask a prospective mediator. The second part of the chapter sets out in some detail ethical standards to which mediators and lawyers should subscribe. The next chapter explores and analyses the fourteen most common barriers to success encountered in mediation and provides useful suggestions on how to overcome them using everyday examples.

The first part of Chapter 6 examines that critical point at the end of the mediation process when there will or will not be agreement. The elements of a good agreement are described in detail. The chapter concludes with some thoughts on how to improve any agreement and what happens if no agreement is reached.

And the final chapter reviews fourteen different types of disputes to highlight the fact that the chances of success may be improved considerably if mediation of these disputes is approached with these differences in mind. Detailed case studies are used to further illustrate these points.

Appendix A is a glossary of ADR terms referred to from time to time throughout the book. Appendix B is a "typical" agreement to mediate. It sets out each party's expectations of the other, and describes the rules and process. The importance of the agreement to mediate cannot be underestimated, and it must be read carefully by the parties before the mediation. If properly prepared, the agreement has the potential of ensuring that the mediation gets off on a good footing. Appendix C reprints two codes of ethics for mediators.

This book is the result of my experience in mediating over 800 cases during the past three years in a pilot project jointly led by the Ontario Court General Division and the Attorney-General of Ontario. As one of two full-time mediators in the project, the material in this book comes from real life examples taken from every type of case imaginable, as well as informal discussions with disputants and their lawyers. But they are composite cases disguised to respect the confidentiality of the actual people. Whenever possible I have used examples to illustrate how the principles of mediation and negotiation apply in practice in an attempt to demystify the process.

While the book describes various techniques from my own experience, the learning I have acquired over the years and from my good fortune at being involved in a project which allowed me to mediate hundreds of different disputes, I have attempted throughout the book to approach the subject in a completely non-dogmatic way. I believe I have become more effective as a mediator by approaching the subject in a straightforward manner, free of the strictures imposed by slavish adherence to the so-called rules. In mediation and negotiation there is no right and wrong, only better—because well-negotiated agreements respond fully to all the requirements of both parties. I hope that this book will help readers enrich any future negotiations and mediations they may participate in and empower them to take hold of processes designed to achieve maximum self-determination.

ACKNOWLEDGEMENTS

A great many people helped me to write this book and I want to thank them. By having the foresight to create the pilot project which provided the opportunity for me to learn and test my ideas, my thanks to the Attorney-General, the government of Ontario, and the Hon. Roy McMurtry, Chief Justice of the Ontario Court of Appeal; Ben Hoffman, my teacher and early mentor, who got me excited about the possibilities five years ago; Magnus Verbrugge, my researcher who worked tirelessly, always with a smile and always on time, despite some short deadlines; Ron Edwards and Nick Purdon whose deft editing often revealed nuggets among the dross; Simon Chester for providing guidance relating to the brave new world of publishing; Stanley Beck, Justices George Adams, Jim Farley, and Warren Winkler for much appreciated support and encouragement during the past three years; my editor at John Wiley & Sons Canada, Ltd, Karen Milner, who took my idea and ran with it and worked hard to accommodate my occasional concerns—she has been a pleasure to deal with; Elizabeth McCurdy at Wiley; Michael Silver, my colleague whose insight and good humour during pre- and post-mediation debriefings has meant a lot to me over the last three years; and my sons Jamie and Norman Patrick who have supported me spiritually. I am also fortunate to have friends like Judith Purcell, Carl Copeland, Nadine Rubin, Hugh MacKenzie, Antge Faulkner, and Kelly Rodgers, whose editorial advice is much appreciated. Pat Hayes provided generous word-processing support.

DISPUTE RESOLUTION METHODS COMPARED

A HANDY REFERENCE TABLE

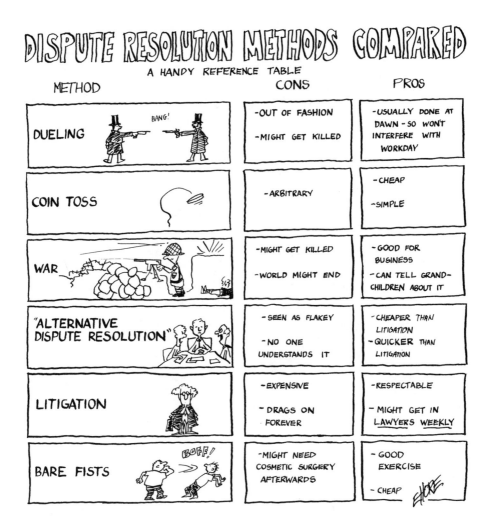

METHOD		CONS	PROS
DUELING	BANG!	-OUT OF FASHION -MIGHT GET KILLED	-USUALLY DONE AT DAWN - SO WON'T INTERFERE WITH WORKDAY
COIN TOSS		-ARBITRARY	-CHEAP -SIMPLE
WAR		-MIGHT GET KILLED -WORLD MIGHT END	-GOOD FOR BUSINESS -CAN TELL GRAND-CHILDREN ABOUT IT
"ALTERNATIVE DISPUTE RESOLUTION"		-SEEN AS FLAKEY -NO ONE UNDERSTANDS IT	-CHEAPER THAN LITIGATION -QUICKER THAN LITIGATION
LITIGATION		-EXPENSIVE -DRAGS ON FOREVER	-RESPECTABLE -MIGHT GET IN LAWYERS WEEKLY
BARE FISTS	BOFF!	-MIGHT NEED COSMETIC SURGERY AFTERWARDS	-GOOD EXERCISE -CHEAP

INTRODUCTION

A stranger has come to town. The name is Mediation. Actually, a new family: Alternate Dispute Resolution (ADR). Mediation is a dispute resolution process that employs a neutral, third party to assist disputing parties in negotiating a mutually satisfactory outcome to their dispute which meets their respective needs, intervening whenever necessary to move the process forward.

Alternate Dispute Resolution (ADR) is a term used loosely to describe historically non-traditional processes involving negotiation or assisted negotiation such as mediation, conciliation, facilitation and fact finding as well as more intrusive, directive forms of dispute resolution including arbitration, early neutral evaluation, and mini-trials.

ADR is changing the way disputes are resolved for three important reasons: cost, timelines, and control.

You, the consumer, have become a very well-informed and demanding bunch. You are no longer content to go along passively with whatever your lawyer decides or leave your fate to a decision imposed by a judge after a lengthy and expensive trial. You want to get involved. You want alternatives. Companies must now, more than ever, due to competitive pressures, contain costs and provide customer satisfaction.

ADR is not a flavour of the month—a here today, gone tomorrow phenomenon. Why? Because it works!

• Disputing parties who are properly prepared love it because they are involved in the process every step of the way and especially in the most important part of that process: the decision on how the dispute will be resolved.

- Court administrators like it because it lessens the number of cases that go to trial.
- Judges like it because it reduces their caseloads and reflects well on the justice system which is under increasing stress and is not working very well.
- Companies involved in a lot of litigation like it because they get faster, less costly results which frees employees to deal with productive business. The money saved goes straight to the bottom line.
- Some better lawyers who are client driven like it because they realize the tremendous human, financial, and lost opportunity costs of litigation.
- Governments and their courts' administrators like it because it saves money—good news for their electorate.

The question is whether you will be welcomed with open arms or treated with reserve, coolness or hostility. While mediating in the General Division of the Ontario Court, I encountered all of these reactions. In the words of George Bernard Shaw, "Critics leave no turn unstoned." However, this is changing because the word is out that ADR works. You, the public are starting to demand alternatives to litigation because you now know there is a better, less costly way.

But the concepts of mediation and other Alternate Dispute Resolution procedures are relatively new. The material in this book is the result of my experience in mediating over 800 cases during the past three years in a pilot project jointly led by the Ontario Court General Division and the Ministry of the Attorney-General (Ontario). Litigants in Ontario will have to quickly become familiar with the concept of mediation. Attorney-General Charles Harnick has declared the pilot project a resounding success and has announced that starting in 1997, all civil cases begun after that date in Ontario must as a first resort attempt mediation before proceeding through the court system to trial unless a special exemption is obtained. There is much speculation that several other provinces are considering following Ontario's lead. In any event, whether mediation is mandatory or voluntary, litigants are becoming increasingly sold on the concept and are instructing their lawyers to explore mediation before resorting to a lawsuit.

Daily, during the past three years, I have observed amazing qualitative differences in the way parties and their lawyers approach mediation—their familiarity with the process, their level of preparation and skill. Perhaps most importantly and of greatest concern to me, are the differing results that flow from such unequal performances. Too many mediations occur where the participants, unfamiliar with the process, sit on their hands and let their lawyers joust back and forth, point by counterpoint. The participants then look expectantly at me to hand down a decision despite the fact that I have told them that mediation is not about getting a decision on who is right or who is wrong. I think to myself, "this is about where things were when we started." While not always the case, it occurs too frequently that the participants and lawyers alike from both parties are unfamiliar with and unprepared for the process. Unfortunately, the results of these mediations are often far less satisfactory than they would otherwise be if everyone understood the process better and came prepared to participate fully.

Mediation, if misunderstood, will quickly acquire a reputation as yet another hurdle to overcome in an already burdensome and expensive legal process. A mediator is not a judge and does not adjudicate. The parties have not given him the authority or power to do so. The mediator and the mediation process need not be regarded with suspicion. Why? Because you (the party)—*not* the mediator and *not* the lawyers—are in charge together with your opponent. You create the agreement based upon *what will work for you*. Mediation is a process which optimizes each party's ability to be heard and to consider the other party's point of view. Mediation is not about vanquishment, public humiliation or complete and total victory; it is consensual agreement based on the merits of each party's case as perceived by *them*.

Much has been written about mediation and ADR with the focus on training mediators and lawyers. There appears to be a growth industry emerging on training would-be mediators. An ADR language is developing. While I wholeheartedly endorse the concept of professionally trained and competent mediators and lawyers, I have an equally strong concern that in our rush to embrace and raise these groups to professional status, we will lose sight of what mediation is all about. It is about giving you (disputants) the means to resolve your own conflicts, no matter how complex they may be.

The key to understanding mediation is realizing that it is nothing more than assisted negotiation between parties in a dispute, with the emphasis on negotiation. Approaching mediation as a negotiation will remove any misplaced mystique and allow you to hone in on the essence of succeeding in mediation. The "knock" we hear all the time against mediation is that it is too "soft and fuzzy." This is only so if the parties fail to understand that it is a negotiation on the merits and if they are not prepared to confront reality. While polite, some of the best mediations in my experience have resembled Australian Rules Football rather than a tea party. Negotiation, as we will see in Chapter 1, is the cornerstone of ADR.

 # NEGOTIATION

The wide panoply of ADR processes appears confusing at first blush. So many different options. Which one should I select? It is useful to view these ADR processes as spectra or continua where the parties have increasingly less control over the outcome. Along with relinquishing control comes increased costs and time consumed.

While we look at these processes in some detail in Chapter 2, What Is ADR?, it should be remembered that despite all the so-called ADR options on offer, the core of ADR consists of three: Negotiation, Mediation, and Arbitration. If you understand that mediation is just negotiation with a twist (the addition of a mediator), there are only two: Negotiation and Arbitration.

The other important difference to bear in mind is that by using arbitration, mini-trial, and litigation, the parties hand over control of the process and the decision to others. In the words of Blanche Dubois in *A Streetcar Named Desire*, they become "dependent on the kindness of strangers."

The central theme of this book is that this is a highly undesirable state of affairs unless all else has failed. In handing the decision-making authority to others, there are only two very narrow possibilities: you either win or lose. That is a situation to be avoided, if possible. And it is possible, very possible.

The ADR spectrum looks like this:

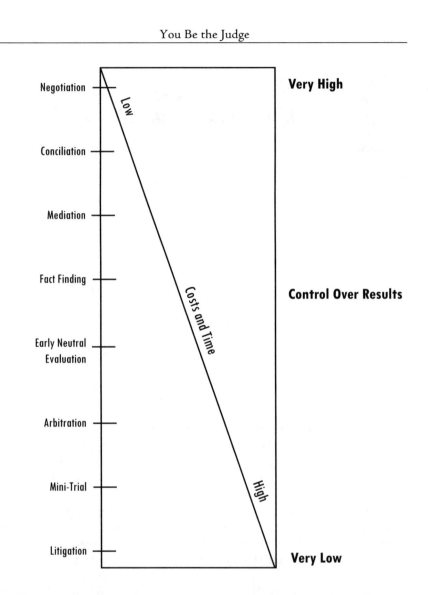

Negotiation, to reiterate, is the lynchpin of ADR. What is negotiation? It is simply direct communication between the parties aimed at resolving their dispute.

Conciliation is an ADR technique which employs a neutral party to act as a go-between among the parties in a failed or troubled negotiation. The conciliator seeks to create more productive conditions leading to a restoration of direct communications between the parties, enabling them to complete their negotiation.

Mediation is negotiation assisted by a neutral, impartial third party who plays an active role in the negotiation.

Fact Finding and *Early Neutral Evaluation* are ADR techniques used most frequently to break deadlocked negotiations. An expert, such as a judge or a person whose knowledge, neutrality, and honesty are unquestioned, is selected by the opponents to provide an objective report or decision on the point(s) in dispute. This affords the disputants an objective method of overcoming their difference of opinion and opens the door for the successful completion of their negotiation.

Negotiation in one form or another plays a significant part in five out of eight ADR processes in the ADR spectrum. Clearly, understanding negotiation and its role in mediation is vital in removing any mystery surrounding mediation. This most useful tool for dispute resolution can then take its place where it belongs: in the forefront of dispute resolution.

WHAT YOU NEED TO KNOW ABOUT NEGOTIATION STYLE

Negotiation is by far the most widely used form of dispute resolution involving direct communication between the parties in conflict. Parties to negotiation are interested in achieving agreement. While Chapter 6 deals with the hallmarks of a good agreement in detail, it is important to have a clear understanding of the goal of negotiation: an agreement or outcome to end the dispute. Agreements should be measurable as being good, bad, or indifferent according to the following criteria:

- efficiency
- fairness
- durablility
- enforceability

An agreement will be efficient and comprehensive if it addresses all parties' identified interests or needs. It will be fair if the parties feel that their case has been heard and that their aspirations have been accommodated. Agreements that do not anticipate common occurrences and contingencies will not endure any more than an agreement in which one side feels taken advantage of or bullied. By enforceable, I mean will the agreement stand up in court? Is it legal and does it comply with applicable laws such as tax regulations?

The ultimate question in negotiation is which style of negotiation will produce an agreement with these characteristics. By understanding both styles, you will have a better appreciation of your own style and that of your opponents. You will also be able to adjust your style if necessary.

Negotiation theory has evolved to the point where at least two kinds of negotiation have been identified: positional or win/lose; and interest-based or win/win.

1. **Positional or Win/Lose Negotiation** assumes that there will be a winner and a loser. The negotiators see themselves as adversaries and resort to strategic behaviour to achieve "success" at the other's expense. The general idea is to get as much as possible. The prevailing climate is one of distrust. Information tends to be shared selectively in order to manipulate and get the "better" of the deal.

2. **Interest-Based or Win/Win Negotiation** or mediation, on the other hand, is based on the objective merits of the case and the underlying interests of each party, measured against realistic alternatives to a negotiated resolution. The approach is one of problem solving based on shared information. The underlying assumption of interest-based negotiation is that both parties will win and will be further ahead if they work to maximize joint gains and minimize potential losses.

When you are trying to decide which style you are dealing with, decide whether it sounds more like haggling with a street vendor or more like the way you talk to yourself. If it sounds like haggling, it's probably positional. If it sounds like the way you talk to yourself, it is probably interest-based. Let us have a look at both these styles in greater detail.

POSITIONAL OR WIN/LOSE NEGOTIATION

Sometimes called distributive or bottom-line negotiation, positional or win/lose negotiation is based on the underlying premise that there is a finite or discrete amount of benefit(s) to be gained—the pie is only so big. Positional negotiators tend to see each other as adversaries. They want to "win," to get as much of the pie as possible, and hope they don't lose.

In win/lose negotiation the emphasis is on winning by demanding the most concessions, getting the other side to move more than you do, and pushing their bottom line. At the same time, your opponents avoid making concessions as much as possible, resist moving as much as possible and in any event, hold fast to their bottom line.

The story of Whiplash Willie comes to mind. It seems Willie's client was craning his neck over the stands in a hockey game and was hit by a passing player, causing severe debilitating and permanent injuries (Whiplash's words, not mine). Whiplash Willie contacted the lawyer for the hockey team and suggested that it would be in everyone's interest to settle the matter. He suggested that he had a figure in mind of $1,000,000. The team's lawyer suggested $1,000. Willie quickly responded, "Let's split it down the middle." The court case is still unfortunately pending. Simply grabbing for as much as you can in negotiation will result in a correspondingly low response. In this case neither Willie nor the team's lawyer bothered to discuss the merits of the case on an objective basis. Overreaching results in a knee-jerk reaction and dismissive low counter-proposal. Often the objective on both sides is to land in the middle. Knowing this, Willie "cut to the chase" in the faint hope of scoring a large settlement, far above what the case was probably worth according to the facts.

In this style of negotiation, the parties seek to:

1. hide their true objectives;
2. create illusions about their priorities and true agendas using diversions and manipulation, including posturing or blaming, even demonizing their opponents in the process;
3. place undue weight on items of little value in the hope of concealing what they really covet and vice versa; and
4. exert power using threats and coercion.

EXAMPLE 1

Suppose two sisters inherit their mother's jewellery. Judith is bequeathed two diamonds and Janet is left two rubies. Judith hates diamonds and loves rubies while Janet is indifferent and loves both diamonds and rubies. Judith may pretend to love diamonds and insist that their value is greater than the rubies in the hope of gaining an advantage. Judith might, for example, suggest that Janet give up both rubies for one of her diamonds, thus hoping to get what she wants under false pretenses.

EXAMPLE 2

I want to get $10,000 for my car, but I ask $25,000. The buyer, playing the same game, offers $5,000. I protest and reluctantly move to $17,500. The buyer curses, asks for a two-year warranty, and offers $7,500. I offer a 30-day warranty and move to $15,000. He starts to leave, saying his final and best offer is $9,000. I tell him to go ahead and leave. I have someone else coming in an hour who said she would pay $15,000, but if he wants the car as is now, without the warranty, I'll take $10,000. The deal is consummated.

The bottom liner A says "I don't fool around, I don't negotiate. My price for the car is $10,000, take it or leave it." B, the positional negotiator, would have trouble with this because that isn't the way the game is supposed to be played and he doesn't trust the other side. B would understand this offer as simply A's extreme demand and start from there. B might therefore offer $5,000. A would say, "I guess you didn't hear me; my price is $10,000." They are deadlocked because B will not "bid against himself." The negotiation is at an end because A and B didn't understand each other.

A basically said, "I don't negotiate. I have an aversion to win/lose negotiation." B thought that was just a ploy and he probably would be right six times out of ten, depending on their culture and understanding of negotiation, but not this time. He expected A to negotiate despite a clear warning to the contrary. Making sure that each side understands the rules governing their negotiation styles sometimes falls to the mediator.

DEADLOCK

Even if both parties possess equal information, in win/lose bargaining it is usually important for one side to "get more" than the other—to *win*. This can be seen in union/management discussions where the union holds out until the last minute "on principle" for another two cents an hour and management won't pay two cents an hour more, also "on principle," to avoid setting a bad precedent for the other companies in the industry. All too often, taking a stance "on principle" is nothing more than a disguise for positional bargaining.

The costs of positional bargaining to each party and to society may be very high:

- The company risks lost production, decreased profits, higher legal costs, management inactivity, bitterness, and potential bankruptcy.

- The workers risk reduced income (strike pay), inactivity, uncertainty, anger, and possible unemployment.

- The union faces increasing pressure to justify its position to the workers and placate their anger caused by increased expenses and reduced income (strike pay, dues). The union ultimately risks reduced membership if the plant closes or goes bankrupt.

- Society as a whole loses. Reduced productivity culminates in lower tax revenue, increased social spending (unemployment insurance and welfare payments), and reduced local spending.

While positional or win/lose negotiation is usually undertaken by a party in the hope of "winning" a greater share of the pie, the negative effects of such a stance may far outweigh the perceived advantages. Positional negotiation commonly results in deadlock. For example, in a strike negotiation both parties play a waiting game hoping the other side will capitulate. The losses in productivity, jobs, and economic activity reverberate throughout the entire economy. Often positional negotiation isn't about one side winning; it's about both sides losing.

THE DEADLY CIRCLE

Win/Lose Negotiation Produces Anger

Parties practising concealment, secrecy, deception, exaggeration, hardball, "chicken" (who will blink first?), the waiting game or scorched earth through protracted litigation or excessive unrealistic demands, will produce significant emotional reactions from the other side. These behaviours will result in accusations, often warranted, that the other party is negotiating in bad faith. Often a refusal to continue the negotiation will result. How many times in labour negotiations do we hear that the parties have broken off talks, or that they are going to court for an injunction, or the government has ordered them to the table and appointed a conciliator? This style of negotiation produces anger, accusation, and intransigence on both sides. This is not an environment conducive to settlement.

Those who practise positional negotiation are all too willing to project their own motives onto the other side. In effect, they demonize them. This happens in litigation all the time.

Vested Interests in Negotiation—The Zero-Sum Game

The effect of the litigation mentality on negotiations cannot be underestimated. Let us examine how this works. By the time mediation occurs in the context of a lawsuit, each party has obtained an opinion from their lawyer that they have a good claim or defence. Now the lawyers have a vested interest in being right. Some become enamoured of and so attached to their legal analysis that they provide overly aggressive opinions. Perhaps they have the mistaken belief that they are dispensing some form of social therapy. What they are doing is digging themselves and their clients in early, often before the case is fully developed. After all, they have only heard one side of the story. It will be difficult for these lawyers to adopt a cooperative problem-solving attitude during negotiations, and it may be difficult for the client to adopt a *change in attitude* to a more conciliatory posture. "I thought you said this case was made in the shade?"

Similarly, accounting, construction, medical, and other experts accustomed to giving evidence, know that in litigation, it's all or nothing: a zero-sum game. It shouldn't be surprising that their reports are prepared in a fashion designed to sustain warfare. Asking them to participate in principled, interest-based negotiations after they have prepared their armour for battle is perhaps requesting a transition worthy of canonization.

Dammit, I'm Right and They're Wrong

This is a position taken by one party in cases where they perceive that justice will not be served by compromise. The party is willing to sacrifice other interests, usually economic, for vindication, face-saving, or just the sheer satisfaction of winning. It may be the principle of the matter.

EXAMPLE

Frank agrees to sell John his restaurant business and the building that houses it for $250,000. John gives Frank a $25,000 deposit to be held by Frank's lawyer in trust pending the transfer of title.

Unbeknown to John, Pete offers Frank $300,000 for the restaurant.

Frank tells John he won't close the deal on some pretext and instructs his lawyer to write a letter setting out numerous technical and highly dubious reasons for his unwillingness to close the deal with John. He claims that the deposit is forfeit. He then sells to Pete.

John sues for the return of the deposit. During the negotiation, John is offered $15,000. His lawyer points out that the lawsuit will probably cost $20,000 and take two to three years to reach a trial date.

Understandably, John is outraged and cannot accept that Frank should be allowed to enrich himself at his expense so unfairly. John wants justice to be done and would "rather pay his lawyer" than see an inequity perpetuated.

On an intellectual level, why should John accept $10,000 less than the full $25,000?

There are a number of reasons best illustrated mathematically.

WIN	LOSE
+ $25,000 – deposit	–$25,000 – deposit
* + $10,000 – Frank's contribution to John's legal fees	–$20,000 – legal costs to his lawyer
–$20,000 – John's legal fees	* –$10,000 – John's contribution to Frank's legal fees
** $15,000 – net gain	–$55,000 – net loss

*In Ontario the courts rarely award the winner more than 50% of his actual legal costs.

** Three years later, nothing has been allowed in John's analysis for the lost value of the money due to inflation over the two- to three-year period he will have to wait for a result. While courts award interest, it is on a very low scale.

Nothing was added for interest but nothing was deducted for the cost of collecting on the judgement from Frank. The cost of collection should not be underestimated, but should be realistically assessed and factored into any analysis involving litigation as an alternative to negotiation. Some lawyers do not see their job as delivering upon a court judgement but merely obtaining it. Experienced successful litigants, some having learned the hard way, know that losers in litigation often go to great lengths to avoid paying judgements. An asset search and realistic assessment of the liquidity of your opponent and costs of collection should always be taken into consideration when weighing the pros and cons of a negotiated or litigated result. Someone who voluntarily agrees to make a payment at an early stage in the litigation (say at the mediation) will be more likely to honour their commitment. Also, precautions may be taken to ensure payment by negotiating for the provision of security, a high interest rate in the event of default, accelerated payments or a "default judgement" to be held in abeyance so long as the terms of the negotiated agreement are honoured. These options are not available from the courts. Judgement must be pursued through the use of bailiffs, sheriffs, and other highly formal legal processes, and is often an ineffective and expensive process.

To resolve this dispute, attention will have to be paid to John's feelings. Frank will have to propose something that recognizes this need—perhaps an apology as well as more money.

BIAS AND SUBJECTIVE EVALUATION

In positional bargaining, which is often conducted in an atmosphere of distrust, exaggeration, and deception are tools of the trade. The parties tend to view proposals put forward by the other side as containing hidden mines or other explosive devices.

Any concessions too readily agreed to will be viewed as having little value. Hard-won concessions will have greater value. Exaggeration is commonplace. For example, "We are prepared to exchange our priceless ruby for the diamond which our expert suggests is almost commercial grade rather than gem quality as you suggest."

In a wrongful dismissal case, an employee terminated "due to a restructuring" was described at various times during the mediation as "an exemplary, valued, highly competent, and hard-working employee" by the lawyer for the employer. Despite these characterizations, the employer's lawyer was rigorously resisting the employee's request for appropriate compensation in lieu of notice. People wedded to positional bargaining apparently do not view their behaviour as irrational.

TIP It should be remembered that inconsistent and contradictory statements like this by the lawyer are given less weight in the negotiation by the other side because lawyers are expected to be positional. Worse, they may have discredited themselves by using harsh and extreme language in the court documents and correspondence. The corollary is also true that statements made directly by one party to the other tend to be heard with more credibility. This should be acknowledged when preparing for any negotiation involving lawyers and parties.

After all is said concerning positional or win/lose negotiation, where the issue is, say, only money and who gets what, the negotiation tends to be distributive. However, there is a principled way to approach these types of negotiations, discussed at length in Chapter 5 on page 97.

INTEREST-BASED OR WIN/WIN NEGOTIATION

As mentioned earlier, in this style of negotiation the parties seek to reach an agreement that is mutually satisfactory without compromising their basic interests. They test the agreement against specific criteria to ensure that it is efficient, fair, durable, and enforceable. Interest-based negotiation presupposes that the parties have both shared and opposing interests.

Personalities are minimized in favour of a cooperative problem-solving approach. The use of threats, power, coercion, and guilt are de-emphasized in favour of probing for, and expressing, underlying concerns, needs, fears, and aspirations. Identifying the real issues, prioritizing them, and communicating each others' points of view are foremost in the parties' minds. Sharing relevant information is critical to the process. When pertinent information is unavailable, it is obtained and shared cooperatively rather than competitively. Wherever possible, the parties seek to employ objective standards and data to test the validity of their assumptions.

When the issues are identified and sufficient information is in hand to make intelligent decisions, the parties generate options and brainstorm in an effort to produce an agreement or resolution that will accommodate the needs of all parties to the greatest extent possible. They strive to create value whenever possible, thus expanding opportunities for agreement. During this process, the parties constantly evaluate options against their best-case scenarios or their walk-away position (WAP). As an aid to testing the realism of their best-case scenerio, they review their worst-case scenario.

In interest-based negotiations, the parties prepare for and conduct the negotiation by:

- Reviewing their own needs, goals, aspirations, fears, and prioritizing them.

- Listening very carefully to what is being said for clues that will help create value, overcome misunderstanding, and ensure that the other side "feels heard." *Listening is not simply waiting for an opportunity to speak.*

- Defining the dispute as a common problem which they will resolve by working together, rather than by having someone else impose a result upon them that may not satisfy either party.

BEST-CASE SCENARIO OR WALK-AWAY POSITION

During any negotiation or mediation, the parties should continually and realistically measure any proposals generated against their alternatives.

Most alternatives in serious disputes involve extreme action such as imposing sanctions, going to court, going to war, or some other drastic remedy. On the other hand, an equally valid alternative may be to do nothing because the downside risks of doing anything else are too great, weighed against the likely reward. To properly understand your alternatives in any negotiation, you should complete an exercise which puts a realistic value on them. Don't forget to include the legal, economic, psychological, and human costs to you or your company.

In order to test the realism of your evaluation, look at your worst-case scenario. By looking at the absolutely worst possible outcome, and then working back through various less costly possibilities, you will have performed an extremely useful analytical exercise focused entirely on *your* interests. You will then be in a good position to analyse your opponent's case, create options before and during the negotiation, and evaluate any proposals made.

Next, do an exercise which attempts to replicate as closely as possible the other party's best and worst-case scenarios. This will help you to walk in their shoes and may give you some ideas on how to create value for both sides.

A TYPICAL INTEREST-BASED NEGOTIATION

A developer wants to develop his land bordering a trout stream. Local fishermen and environmentalists are adamantly opposed, claiming that the development will pollute the stream by removing trees and topsoil, causing erosion and creating septic tank run-off.

The developer's position is: I own the land, it is zoned for development and I'm going ahead. The fishermen's position is: The river is an important ecological feature of the region, has been providing generations of fishermen from all over the province with pleasure and must be protected at all costs.

Each has hired lawyers who advise their respective clients that they have a good chance of winning. The fishermen know that if they can delay the development for five years, the developer may go out of business. The developer knows that the fishermen have limited resources and if the stakes get too high, they may fold their tents.

In an interest-based negotiation, the parties will:

1. Commit to resolving the problem on its merits.

2. Carefully review their respective alternatives to a negotiated solution.

3. Explore their interests—that is, their needs and concerns—openly with a view to finding some common ground.

4. Apply objective criteria to test the validity of any interest. For example,

they may agree to use scientific data relating to the impact of a similar development on a similar fishing stream. They might agree to use construction techniques which did not have an adverse environmental impact on other developments.

5. Develop creative options which incorporate their mutual interests and reduce their conflicting interests as much as possible.

6. Measure these options against their alternatives, and if they are better than they could otherwise do by employing their alternatives, enter into an agreement and resolve the dispute.

WHAT STYLE OF NEGOTIATION BEST SUITS MEDIATION?

Mediators generally promote interest-based negotiation over positional bargaining. However, negotiators and mediators should be familiar with both types because it is as natural to be competitive as it is to be cooperative. Channelling these natural instincts productively is the task of the mediator and is the reason why mediators are invaluable in assisting the parties to avoid deadlock.

Although you should be familiar with both styles for identification purposes, you need not revert to positional negotiation simply because your opponent chooses to negotiate in that style. If you have properly prepared and analysed your position, you will know whether or not to enter into an agreement without resorting to positional tactics. You may even teach the other side a new and improved negotiation style that benefits you both.

REACTIVE DEVALUATION

This term refers to the natural tendency to ascribe less value to concessions made or offered by your opponent than to concessions they will not make. An example of this is offering outplacement assistance or a letter of reference in a wrongful dismissal negotiation *before* either item was requested. This concept in and of itself is a good reason for not *"cutting to the chase"* or rushing to table your bottom line early in the negotiation. It may seem time-consuming to explore fully all possible areas of the agreement; however, experience suggests that the time is well spent and the chances of reaching agreement are greatly increased if you do.

In contrast, options or proposals for settlement which are seen as coming from a neutral party are often given correspondingly more weight. This is why it may be better to float a settlement concept through the mediator without claiming authorship.

In the context of positional negotiation, it is perfectly understandable that reactive devaluation will occur. Remember that in positional negotiation we strive to hide our interest in certain items so as to devalue them in the eyes of our opponent, and we puff up and feign interest in keeping that which we are happy to unload.

IMPASSE IN NEGOTIATION

The Whack-Um Game

Impasse is similar to the game you often see at fall fairs called "Whack-Um." You have a hammer and must whack the furry little creatures into their holes. As fast as you do, others pop up.

Similarly, in negotiations, just as the parties approach closure and all the issues seem resolved, another issue or demand pops up, sometimes leading to accusations of bad faith. While this may be the case, a more likely explanation, in my experience, is that the party raising the demands has a particular interest, fear, or aspiration which has not been sufficiently addressed. Rather than engage in vituperative exchanges which may cause regression or deadlock, it is important to uncover the difficulty and address it properly. It is here that the skilful mediator earns his keep by preventing the parties from backsliding while working to uncover the real problem.

Diagnosing the Problem

The best way to break an impasse is to understand what is causing it:

- Careful analysis and dissection of the issue that is preventing progress should reveal whether a ploy is being used or a more fundamental problem exists.
- Is there something missing from the negotiation? Go back to the fundamentals. Is there a party missing from the table for example?
- Has the party at the table run out of authority but is unwilling to admit it? Is there a senior lawyer pulling the strings of the junior over the phone?
- Is there a corporate policy at stake, or the fear of setting a costly precedent?
- Has some external event occurred that has caused a change of climate? Disputes are dynamic. The passage of time and the occurrence of external events may well influence attitudes at the table. For example, exposure to lawsuits can lead to a determination to seek creditor or bankruptcy protection as Union Carbide did in Bhopal, India, after the massive environmental disaster, or Dow Corning with the breast implants, or certain religious orders accused of wide-scale physical and sexual abuse.

- What purpose does keeping the dispute alive serve for the reluctant party? Consider emotional issues to determine if psychological interests have been appropriately addressed. (See the section on Anger in Chapter 5.)

- Is one of the parties financially or emotionally drained? Have they conceded so much that they are having second thoughts about their alternatives? Is taking their chances in court looking better all the time? They may be up against the wall. If this has happened, the other side had better look long and hard at their own best-case scenario or walk-away position.

- Is there a glaring element that has been overlooked in the resolution mix such as a press release that will "give back" some face?

Additional Strategies To Break Impasse

Defer to Another Authority or Method:

- a neutral expert;

- use Early Neutral Evaluation, a fact finder, or some other ADR technique;

- draw straws or flip coins.

Disengage from the Negotiation:

- for a short break, a coffee, some fresh air, a walk, a phone call, or to meet privately with the mediator who may have some ideas;

- for a longer period to send a message, allow each party to accumulate more information, cool down, or consider alternatives;

- to undertake activities that might have a profound effect on shifting a party's walk-away position, for example: launching a lawsuit, starting a public relations campaign, or making a strategic alliance.

Indirect Confrontation

Use the mediator to give voice to your opinion on the untenability of your opponent's position. The mediator should possess the skill to present the information in a way that doesn't jeopardize his relationship with your opponent.

Some of the most common points that may come up include a lack of awareness by either party of the financial and emotional toll a lawsuit may exact, or a proposal may be too unwieldy or impractical due to flaws in a party's logic or assumptions.

Unproductive Tactics Or Behaviour

If you detect any of the behaviours or strategies (discussed at length in Chapter 5, Barriers to Success) and wish to avoid direct confrontation, take the mediator into your confidence. The mediator may be able to end the behaviour by revealing it in the safety of a private meeting with the other side. The mediator may make the observation as hers, rather than yours.

Something Rather Than Nothing

When all is said and done and everything has been tried, partial closure on certain issues should be examined. What about a partial solution, a trade or compromise? It may be better than nothing.

Humour

While humour is a dangerous tool, used discreetly, humour may have a remarkable effect on breaking impasse or at least the ice. I am reminded of the story of the ivy league graduate during his first job interview with the V.P. of Human Relations at MegaTech Corp.

Applicant: "I'm assuming a starting salary of $150,000."

V.P.: "You will also be pleased to know you'll be entitled to a BMW every two years, the executive pension top up, stock options, medical package, and a six-week vacation annually."

Applicant: "You're kidding."

V.P.: "You started it."

Other Strategies

Other process options may be available to deal with outstanding issues. If the dispute has been refined through trades or compromise on one issue, it may make sense to refer that issue to a trusted higher authority, such as a neutral expert or arbitrator, who could put the matter to rest with a binding or non-binding decision.

LITIGATION MODE IS NOT NEGOTIATION

Lawyers and their clients are often victims of the adversarial system. This system encourages people to marshal all the facts, law, and witnesses in their favour while at the same time, devaluing and minimizing their opponents' arguments and witnesses. All of this is done in preparation for a trial where each side places their admittedly slanted views before a judge whose only option is to choose between the two.

During this process it is not surprising that the lawyers and their clients' convictions are reinforced positively towards their case and negatively towards their opponents'. The tendency is to demonize your opponent in litigation and inflate your chances of success. Why not? Losing is a fearsome prospect.

If the litigation route is chosen, it is easy to understand that less time will be devoted to understanding the opponents' perspective. In litigation, information is not readily shared, which often leads to erroneous assumptions. Each party has limited access to the information used by the other. Since it is precisely this information which assists us in understanding our opponents' perspective, it is understandable that parties overvalue their own case and denigrate their opponents'.

The opposite of overvaluation, but equally harmful, is undervaluation, or loss aversion. For example, a municipal council that is torn between anti-smoking activists and the board of trade representing restaurants, might refer the matter to a court or an inquiry rather than risk the fallout if they simply put the matter to a vote.

Risk aversion is also at play when a party evaluates its chances of winning or losing. Parties to negotiation have different tolerances when it comes to being able to withstand a loss. An individual victim of medical malpractice with limited financial means may place a completely different value on accepting a modest offer of settlement to obtain certainty and avoid the costly possibility of losing, than would a government agency being sued by a company over alleged bias by an adjudicator in a regulatory proceeding.

Since over 95% of all lawsuits settle before a trial, it seems bizarre that negotiations should be conducted in the litigation mode rather than adopting the more open interest-based, problem-solving approach. If the goal of negotiation is indeed an efficient, fair, durable, and enforceable agreement, this approach has got to change.

Quite apart from the litigation mindset that produces awkward, positional, and often unproductive negotiation, it is apparent that the legal system is in crisis. While litigation is and will remain a legitimate method of dispute resolution, it is now recognized by many that it cannot be the exclusive or even the pre-eminent method. Given the increased bellicosity of society, the complexity of the issues, technology advances, and huge costs of litigation (estimated on average at just under $40,000 per party in Ontario), it is not surprising that there is almost unanimous agreement that the system must become more accessible, efficient and timely, as well as less expensive.

Is mutual satisfaction possible in a negotiation when the parties are in litigation mode? Not likely, due to such tactics as application of force and threats. The usual scenario is that settlements come late, after years of litigation. Compromises are reached usually at the courtroom door because neither side is totally confident in their best-case scenario, and because they have not really been negotiating. They have been *bluffing* and it's now show time.

POWER IN NEGOTIATION

Power dynamics are inevitable in negotiation. But the use of power in negotiation is often misunderstood. Power does not emanate simply from who has the most resources. Often big money, big business or government are vulnerable in negotiation for that very reason. However, anyone involved in a dispute will be well advised to take stock of the power inventory on both sides of the table.

Money, status, authority, favourable legal precedent, ability to influence opinion or advancement, and access to data are all sources of power—raw power. More subtle, but every bit as potent, is the ability to affect economic interests through, for example, office politics or adverse press coverage. Often the most powerful negotiator is the one with little or nothing to lose. The demented psycho/hijacker or the debtor who has no money commands a great deal of power. Perhaps one of the most overlooked sources of power is *negotiating skill.*

Negotiating power derives from many sources including the way you approach the negotiation, your demeanour, level of preparation, your ability to understand the other side's needs as well as your own, and your skill and creativity at crafting solutions that create added value. Negotiating power may well offset or blunt raw power.

Power tactics may also be used on the mediator. Attempts made to win over, manipulate, or curry favour with the mediator should be avoided. These will backfire, antagonizing the other party and make the mediator uncomfortable. Concentrate your efforts on persuading your opponents. Obviously, you don't want to alienate the mediator. However, he will not be offended if you direct your attention and effort to the other side of the table, appearing to ignore him.

Power Imbalances

Negotiation conducted skilfully is, if anything, empowering; but if it becomes clear during the negotiation that power is being *abused,* the issue should be addressed and rectified or the process discontinued. In my opinion, undue preoccupation with power imbalance before it becomes manifest unnecessarily burdens the process. Negotiation is voluntary. Unless the parties reach agreement, their interests remain unaffected and unencumbered by any obligations. They are always at liberty to leave the table. Why anticipate problems that may not exist?

The presence of a mediator ensures an added degree of fairness, civility, and appropriate behaviour. However, mediators who see themselves as "power balancers" and feel justified in tilting the playing field based on their own subjective assessment of "power imbalance," run the risk of losing all credibility and being open to a charge of unethical behaviour. Developing a strong walk-away alternative is perhaps the best protection against so-called power imbalances.

This is not to say that if there is a perceived problem, abuse of power should not be raised for discussion by a party or by the mediator in a neutral and ethical fashion. The mediator should not, however, be expected to champion a particular party where power is being misapplied. The mediator may have a duty in these circumstances to end the process if the behaviour or abuse continues.

NEGOTIATING TIPS

Leave Them Better Than You Found Them

- One of your objectives throughout the negotiation should be to end the discussions on a note that is positive whether or not an agreement is reached at that particular session. If you have this objective in mind throughout your discussions, you will avoid most of the pitfalls related to unproductive behaviour.

Be Assertive, Not Rude

- Don't compromise your core interests. If agreeing to a certain demand is not acceptable, say no. "John, giving you a five-year guarantee is just not negotiable." A rule I follow is to consider whether I would use those words or tone in addressing my grandfather or grandmother.

Don't Complain Or Explain

- Avoid criticism and blame. Nothing drives a wedge into the negotiation or pushes your opponent away faster than pointing fingers and personalizing the dispute. Accusing your opponent of causing the dispute is unproductive. Do not react to blame with a defensive explanation.
- Treat the problem as one that you both share. "I would rather not be in this lawsuit. I hope you feel the same way."

Send Reinforcing Positive Messages

• Throughout the negotiation, look for ways to demonstrate your good faith and commitment. Unless your core interests are affected, build agreement without always looking for reciprocity. This sets the tone and will create momentum.

• Don't hamstring yourself by declaring your bottom line prematurely. All you are doing is limiting your options, including those you may not have considered. You are also declaring you don't have much respect for the other side's point of view or their ability and that of the mediator to develop creative options.

Negotiate In Good Faith

• Negotiate in good faith and insist on similar behaviour from your opponents. My own guiding principle is the biblical golden rule "Do unto others as you would have them do unto you."

• If information is being withheld that is so critical that refusal to disclose it amounts to deception, misrepresentation, or an attempt to gain an unfair advantage, I will end the mediation. One of the important criteria of a good agreement is that it be fair. Furthermore, an abiding tenet of principled negotiation is that the parties will seek a mutually satisfactory outcome based on open and complete communication.

End the Negotiation On a Positive Note

• Even if you can't reach an agreement, if at all possible, table a comprehensive offer or proposal. This demonstrates good faith and gives the other side something tangible to chew on for the next session.

2 WHAT IS ADR?

THE NEED FOR CHANGE

A lawsuit, or any other form of dispute resolution which involves having a decision imposed by a third party, is a crude way to settle differences. Society is changing; people are seeking more sophisticated results than those available through litigation, outcomes that accommodate many competing, often conflicting, interests in ways that do not leave either side bludgeoned, bankrupt or, as in most cases, exhausted and dissatisfied by the cost and length of time involved in getting a decision.

There is a widespread demand for better and earlier results for all concerned than is possible through traditional methods of dispute resolution. Courts, boards or tribunals have their origins in primitive societies where combat, war, trial by ordeal, and royal decree were highly regarded as tools for governing and settling disputes. These are blunt instruments which spawned warlike slogans such as "might is right," "the spoils go to the victor," "take no prisoners," and "scorched earth policy." In 1997 I still hear these phrases used every day by some lawyers.

Our system of justice derives generally from the thinking of medieval lawyers and ancient ecclesiastical scholars who spoke in simplistic terms to simple people—terms such as right and wrong, good and evil, saint and sinner, heaven and hell, damnation or salvation. It is not surprising that the justice system and the thinking that created it devised a process which could produce only two results: win or lose. This process takes from two to five years or more to achieve a result at an average cost of $38,000 per party involved, according to the recently released *Final Report of the Ontario Civil Justice Review 1997.*

It isn't the lawyers' or judges' fault that we've come to this crisis; it's the medieval adversarial system they must work within. It is a system which has grown not like topsy, but as a result of periodic "reforms" every thirty or so years over the last five centuries which, because of the tinkering, resembles a contraption out of the movie *Chitty Chitty Bang Bang,* a Rube Goldberg machine. It is a system in which, as one experienced litigant described, one feels more like the way suspected witches must have felt if they floated when thrown in the water. If they floated, they were said to be guilty and burnt at the stake; if they drowned, they were innocent, but dead.

The bench, bar, and government have recognized that this state of affairs cannot continue. Much of the credit for these calls for change must go to the public which has made no secret of its sense of alienation from a system supposedly designed to be a pillar of civilized society.

A large part of the change is mediation, and Alternative Dispute Resolution (ADR) processes generally, whose central theme is self-determination—giving back to the parties control over their destiny and the outcome of their dispute whenever possible. The simple win/lose dichotomy is no longer practical or useful. Disputes are no longer straightforward matters of right or wrong, black or white. If anything, most disputes are a complex kaleidoscope of grey.

Throughout the book, references to litigation are frequently made. Since ADR and particularly mediation are often referred to as alternatives to litigation, it is worth examining the steps in the litigation process. I see ADR and mediation not only as alternatives to litigation but as steps that can be taken at any time during the litigation process. For example, there is nothing to prevent disputing parties from selecting mediation before starting a lawsuit or for that matter, agreeing to a mediation or arbitration during the course of the litigation. In fact, this is occurring with more frequency as the public becomes aware of these options.

What follows is a general outline of the steps in the litigation process, without attempting to be exhaustive.

THE LITIGATION PROCESS

Step 1

Claimant (referred to as the plaintiff), having received no satisfaction through conventional discussions and negotiation, seeks legal advice. A preliminary opinion is given by the lawyer that the case is worth pursuing. Discussions may ensue with the opponent's lawyer. If the matter is not resolved, it proceeds to Step 2.

Step 2

Claimant's lawyer prepares a claim, called a Statement of Claim, succinctly setting out the reasons for the claim and the relief sought, usually money damages. This document is served on the opponent (defendant).

Step 3

The defendant consults his lawyer who may negotiate with the claimant's lawyer and resolve the matter. If not, the defendant is required to prepare and file a Statement of Defence setting out why the claimant is not entitled to the relief sought.

Step 3A

In 1997 in Ontario, all lawsuits will be required to attend a mediation within sixty days of the filing of the Statement of Defence or seek an exemption from a court official. The parties will choose a mediator from an approved roster and the rules governing the mediation, fees, and mediator conduct will be supervised by the Ministry of the Attorney-General, the courts, and local bar by means of a committee.

Step 4

Both parties exchange affidavits cataloguing all relevant documents relating to the claim and defence. This process is called Documentary Discovery.

Step 5

The parties must attend before an official called a special examiner with their lawyers for cross-examinations on all matters and documents relevant to the claim and defence. This is the oral part of Discoveries. One to two years may have elapsed since Step 1. A transcript of the questions and answers is made available to both parties.

Step 6

Experts' reports may at this stage be obtained by both sides, each expert supporting the contentions of their employers.

Step 7

The lawyers set the matter down for trial and declare they are ready to proceed with the trial.

Step 8

The lawyers (rarely with clients) appear before a Pretrial Judge who will not hear the case if it proceeds to trial. The lawyers give a brief summary of their cases at their best, as well as rebutting their opponents' contentions. The judge, after forty-five minutes to an hour, exhorts them to settle and provides guidance by way of an advisory opinion on how he or she would rule in the case.

Step 9

The trial will take place lasting an average of two to four days. The parties, their experts, and any other relevant witnesses will give their evidence before the judge under oath and be cross-examined in an effort by the opponent to minimize the impact of their evidence.

Step 10

The judge will render a decision favouring the claimant or defendant. If the claimant succeeds, a judgement will be issued in his favour ordering the relief deemed appropriate by the judge. If the defendant succeeds, the plaintiff's case will be dismissed. The successful party will usually be awarded costs to be paid by the losing party. These are assessed on a scale which results in only partial recovery of the total legal bill, usually about 50% of the actual cost. The loser is responsible to pay his costs as well as those awarded to the winner.

Step 11

The losing party will generally have the right to appeal to the Divisional Court or Court of Appeal. Enforceability of the judgement may be held in abeyance pending the appeal which may take another one to three years to be heard.

Throughout the process either party may bring a motion before a judge under the rules to compel, for example, a reluctant party to provide information or perhaps security for legal costs, to name but two. These motions, while less formal, are still before a judge and are based on affidavit evidence which entitles the other side to a further cross-examination.

The Litigation Process

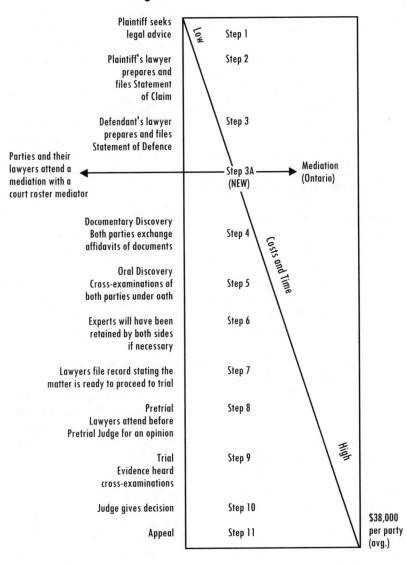

Plaintiff seeks legal advice	Step 1
Plaintiff's lawyer prepares and files Statement of Claim	Step 2
Defendant's lawyer prepares and files Statement of Defence	Step 3
Parties and their lawyers attend a mediation with a court roster mediator	Step 3A (NEW) → Mediation (Ontario)
Documentary Discovery Both parties exchange affidavits of documents	Step 4
Oral Discovery Cross-examinations of both parties under oath	Step 5
Experts will have been retained by both sides if necessary	Step 6
Lawyers file record stating the matter is ready to proceed to trial	Step 7
Pretrial Lawyers attend before Pretrial Judge for an opinion	Step 8
Trial Evidence heard cross-examinations	Step 9
Judge gives decision	Step 10
Appeal	Step 11

Low

Costs and Time

High

$38,000 per party (avg.)

The following is a typical example of a case proceeding through the litigation process.

Case Study

A retailer with several outlets, which declared bankruptcy in the early 1990s leaving its major supplier high and dry, owed several hundred thousand dollars. The supplier attended the various meetings of creditors, spent considerable money searching out the facts and concluded the retailer had taken several shipments of goods in its dying days using the proceeds improperly to repay family members and other preferred creditors at the expense of the supplier. The matter was aggravated by the fact that both the retailer and supplier were family businesses and the presidents had done business together profitably for twenty-five years.

The supplier sued the retailer alleging fraud and made personal allegations of deceitful and fraudulent behaviour against the president and his family. The lawsuit progressed normally through the early phases, the lawyers examining the evidence in their clients' possession that would prove or disprove the allegations and reporting their conclusions to their clients. Each party made the appropriate documentary disclosure (in this case four large binders of documents were exchanged). Oral discoveries took place and each president was thoroughly cross-examined.

Two and a half years after the suit was launched, the matter came before a judge for a pretrial. Each lawyer spent about an hour trying to convince the judge that their client did or did not intentionally defraud the other. Numerous cases were cited and references were made to the transcripts of the cross-examination.

The judge listened patiently and when they were finished, asked if there had been any settlement discussions. No, there had not. Each party was adamant. He asked whether mediation had been suggested or considered. No, it had not been. However, both counsel had had good success with mediation in the past year and said they would discuss the matter with their clients. The judge wisely refrained from providing them with an opinion as to who, in his opinion, would win the lawsuit, which could have added considerable wind to one party's sails making negotiation more difficult.

More than thirty months had elapsed since the start of the lawsuit and each party had paid over $10,000 each to their lawyers. They were looking at a further year to eighteeen months before a trial date, a five-day trial, and a further $20,000 to $25,000 in legal fees. The two presidents agreed to attend a mediation. A month after the pretrial, the lawyers had completed their mediation briefs, prepared their clients and were able to attend the mediation.

During the mediation, the two old business associates were at pains to listen to each other's point of view. The retailer had been outraged to read the allegations of fraud. The supplier explained his concerns at the timing of the orders. Most of the mediation dealt with explanations of each other's point of view, what had been happening in the retailer's business, how the business had come apart suddenly, and so on. The retailer further explained that the bankruptcy had left him and his family with very little, and what little was left had been invested in starting over.

They agreed to settle their differences in a highly creative way. The supplier agreed to provide the retailer's new enterprise with certain goods the retailer could not obtain elsewhere on a COD basis. The retailer agreed to take a minimum amount of product per month over the next three years, thereby guaranteeing that the supplier would receive the amount lost in the bankruptcy. At the end, they were exchanging stories about their families and looking forward to resuming their business relationship.

The mediation took five hours. Each lawyer charged $250 per hour. Assuming three hours for preparation, each party paid their lawyer $2,000. Had I not been provided free of charge by the province and charged, say, $250 per hour, the mediation with preparation of two hours, would have cost an additional $1,750, each party paying $875. The entire matter was settled for under $3,000 per party. Furthermore, it was settled in a way that was far more elegant than a court judgement, which would have meant an end to the relationship and cost each party an additional $20-25,000. Had the supplier won, the resulting judgement would probably have been unenforceable and uncollectible.

This case study demonstrates that in most cases, a negotiated result is preferable to litigation. And, the following illustrates what would have happened had other forms of ADR been used at the outset:

- Had the parties been able to avoid litigation and negotiated face to face without a mediator or the lawyers, they would have had their result two and a half years earlier and saved collectively $26,000.

- If the parties had arbitrated at the outset, the matter might have been resolved two years earlier at somewhat reduced cost. However, the result would have been either that the arbitrator would have found that the retailer owed the several hundred thousand dollars or he did not. The arbitrator might have awarded costs if the parties gave him the mandate to do that. There would be no creative resolution involving future business and the supplier, and if he won he would be in the unenviable position of attempting to get blood out of a stone.

- In court the judge would be in the same position as the arbitrator, able only to favour one side over the other and to award costs. The difference between the arbitration and court decision is that three additional years would have elapsed and the parties' total legal costs would have approached $60,000.

The truth is, the public is terrified of litigation. The fear factor is exacerbated by horror stories that abound. Everyone has a lawsuit-or lawyer-from-hell story to tell involving themselves, a business associate, a relative, or a neighbour. These stories invariably feature combinations of the following ingredients: horrendous costs, years of delay caused by the other side's scheming, lying, cheating, the overtaxed legal system, lawyers who overcharge, and lawyers who take on a matter and promise victory at the beginning only to change their tune and advise settlement after years of cost and delay.

Whether the stories are true in whole or in part, the time has come, and the opportunity has presented itself through mediation and ADR, to avoid becoming another unhappy storyteller. I, for one, believe the public is ready to embrace ADR, and particularly mediation, once they know more about it.

THE DELAY FACTOR

Delays in the legal system can run to five years in some regions of the country. Historically, the lawyers were given a lot of latitude to decide the pace and progress of the case with little interference from the courts, the theory being that in an adversarial system, undue delay by one side would prompt the other to ask the court to intervene and punish the offender. What happens if both sides are not in a hurry? Nothing. Imagine cases with three or four parties and busy lawyers attempting to coordinate their schedules for a four- or five-day trial. Other reasons for delay often cited are too few judges, antiquated and inefficient scheduling technology, and the number of cases being started.

The judges are starting to assert more authority in this area with the introduction of case management. This system assigns the management of cases to a judge who will presumably be intolerant of undue delay. Hopefully, case management will eliminate at least the most flagrant examples of intentional delay.

THE HISTORICAL CONTEXT

Who do we entrust with the weighty responsibility of resolving our disputes? Lawyers and judges who were once lawyers. Every effort is no doubt made to ensure confidence in our lawyers and judges. However, in North America, judges are either elected or appointed by the government of the day and receive little or no training in judging. Apparently, they are expected to learn on the job. Furthermore, judges hear only what the lawyers decide they should hear. The clients are cut off from the decision maker and are only heard when answering questions put to them by their counsel.

The public is no longer content with being told what to do. People are becoming more cynical and their former confidence in authority and the ability of public institutions to deliver the goods has been eroded. Due to improved standards of education, people are far better equipped to make their own decisions. A major shift is occurring. Modern writers have dubbed this trend a cultural transformation. Consider the following:

- There is a trend to flatten corporate hierarchies in an effort to move decision making closer to the customer.
- Much greater attention is being paid to customer service and satisfaction. Customers are demanding better quality and service because they are more discerning, better educated, more outspoken, and increasingly mobile.
- People are demanding alternatives and a greater voice in decisions that matter a great deal in their lives.
- Individuals and companies are reinventing themselves in shorter and shorter periods. In an age of instant access to information and communication, the idea of waiting even a year or two for a decision, let alone three to five years, is simply not acceptable.

ADR STREET

I see ADR as a village street which ends in a square dominated by an imposing courthouse. The following "shops" line the ADR Street:

Negotiation

The first shop you encounter on your stroll down the street is direct negotiation between the parties. Whatever techniques or strategies are employed, whatever number of parties or the length of time consumed by the process, if it is done well and persistently as we saw in Chapter 1, negotiation or direct communication by the parties has an excellent chance of succeeding.

Mediation

If direct negotiation is not successful, the next stop on the village street is mediation, or assisted negotiation. The parties are assisted in their negotiation by the mediator. The mediator is more than simply a facilitator or conciliator; rather, the mediator is an individual who possesses skill, neutrality, and experience at intervening in difficult disputes assisting the parties to reach agreement. The vast majority of disputes will be resolved if direct

negotiation and mediation are attempted. With each stop along the ADR Street, the likelihood of resolution is greatly increased. In particularly difficult cases, two or three stops may be necessary.

The Mini-Mall

The next stop involves a mini-mall of boutiques with offerings such as Early Neutral Evaluation, Mini-Trial, and Fact Finding. Early Neutral Evaluation essentially involves obtaining an advisory opinion on points in dispute from a neutral expert, judge, ex-judge, or senior lawyer. Mini-Trial is an ADR technique which entails a panel of senior executives, one from each disputant, chaired by a neutral party who hears truncated versions of each party's case and delivers a decision which may be binding or advisory. Fact Finding employs a neutral person of stature to investigate facts in dispute and incorporate the results in a report; the parties agree beforehand whether it will be binding or merely informative. It was used, for example, recently in Ontario to investigate allegations of sexual harassment by an employee against a member of the Ontario government. These processes are often useful during a mediation to resolve an impasse or when mediation fails to produce agreement. Going straight to the mini-mall makes little sense because these processes can be very expensive and minimize the amount of direct input by the parties.

Arbitration

The penultimate stop on the street is arbitration. The arbitration shop is beside the courthouse because it is so similar to going to court. But there are some important differences. While the arbitrator imposes a decision (the award), the parties decide the rules of procedure, rights of appeal, whether or not the arbitration decision will be binding and, most important, who the arbitrator(s) will be.

Rent-A-Judge

Several retired judges now offer services covering the wide spectrum of ADR techniques from mediation through arbitration. Essentially, judges, through years of training and experience at judging, tend to do just that—judge. If what is required is an advisory opinion on the merits of the case or a choice between conflicting experts' reports or views of the law, a wise, judicial, elder statesman may be just the ticket.

Rights Based "Mediation"

Around the corner from ADR Street and slightly off the beaten track is Rights-Based Mediation. This is a brand of ADR whereby the "mediator" provides a view or opinion of the case after hearing the parties and witnesses and reviewing the documents. It looks, smells, and tastes a lot like Early Neutral Evaluation. THIS IS NOT MEDIATION. Why? Because the parties are not central to the process nor are they in control of the outcome. This form of ADR is quite popular with some lawyers and insurance claims adjusters and examiners because it is very similar to the judicial process with which they are most familiar. Their experience is with litigation. As these adjusters, their lawyers, and the public become more familiar and comfortable with true mediation, this form of dispute resolution will decline in popularity.

In rights-based mediation, one side prevails, the other side loses. As a result, one side is usually very unhappy with the outcome. To be fair, it does permit some party involvement, is reasonably quick, and less costly than a trial. But the "winning" party may be encouraged to litigate rather than resolve the matter, and the "loser" may decide to take their chances in court. It is, however, an alternative form of dispute resolution. The point of ADR is to help individuals achieve autonomy in the settlement of their disputes. It is not about having the dispute resolved by others in a well meaning but nevertheless paternalistic fashion, which may or may not reflect the reality of the situation or the real needs of the parties.

Court

It bears repeating that through the use of the various stops along the way well over 95% of all cases settle before they reach the final stop: the courtroom. The question might well be asked if that was so, why get so excited about the benefits of ADR or mediation? The answer lies in the timing of settlements, the reasons for settling, and the kinds of agreements achieved. Most settlements achieved before mediation came on the scene occurred at the courthouse door, years after the start of the lawsuit and thousands of dollars in legal fees later. Rather than efficient, fair, durable, and enforceable agreements, the settlements were usually about shattered illusions, irreparably damaged relationships, lack of funds, and emotional stamina.

Finally, you reach the courthouse—large, austere, imposing and, yes, intimidating. Courts dispense a very important societal product: Justice. All the other shops dwell in the shadow of the courts. No one is above their supervision or authority. The way to the courthouse is never blocked, nor should it be simply because you browsed down ADR street. But this should be your last stop along the ADR Street.

In conclusion, customers will always shop where service and satisfaction can be found, quickly and inexpensively. ADR techniques and particularly mediation, provide this. They allow people to resolve disputes without compromising their basic interests based on the strengths and weaknesses or merits of their case through accommodation, the balancing of expectations, and the use of objective data.

Apart from arbitration, such techniques as Early Neutral Evaluation, Mini-Trial, and Fact Finding are not in widespread use. To put their usefulness in perspective, in over 800 mediations in which I was involved, Early Neutral Evaluation was proposed six times and used twice to good effect in breaking impasse.

MEDIATION IN DETAIL

This book concentrates almost entirely on mediation for several reasons:

- Mediation is the ADR process of choice in the first instance by sophisticated disputants whose direct negotiations have broken down for one reason or another, because it is informal, cost effective, and may be set up quickly.

- Mediation encourages direct participation by the parties, is controlled by them, and still leaves all other ADR options open.

- Success rates are impressive, varying from 60% to 90%, depending on timing, preparation of the participants, and type of dispute.

- Mediation is the ADR process most often imposed by government on disputing parties in their quest to save money.

- Mediation is private and confidential employing a neutral third party (the mediator) who possesses the skill and experience necessary to help disputing parties negotiate an agreement which will meet their respective needs.

- The parties control the process. At the outset, for example, the parties to the dispute exert their control by selecting the mediator.

- The parties also control who will be present during the mediation. They decide with the mediator whether or not to have their lawyers present throughout the process. They decide who will represent them and whether or not to have a spouse or friend along for moral support.

- Perhaps most vitally important, the parties design and create the agreement to end their dispute and tailor it to their needs.

ADVANTAGES OF MEDIATION

Why should individuals involved in a dispute prefer mediation over, say, arbitration or rent-a-judge? The answer lies in several fundamental truths:

- Studies have consistently reported tremendous user satisfaction with mediation. A research report published in the *Harvard Negotiation Journal* (July 1996) reported that a study of 449 cases revealed that mediation settled 78% of them, regardless of whether the parties had been required to mediate by the court or had selected the process voluntarily. The study found that mediation cost far less, took less time, and was found superior to arbitration. The evaluation of the pilot project in which I was involved, where mediation had been court mandated, had similar findings. Contrast this with traditional litigation where winners and losers are generally both dissatisfied at the cost and length of time to get a decision. Losers rarely accept the decision and the winner is generally unhappy because the judgement is never enough.

- You control the timing of the mediation. Time is money.

- You have lived with the dispute since the beginning and know its details intimately, while a judge, or other third party, hears only a limited and truncated version of the dispute before imposing a decision.

- The cost of mediation, especially if done early in a dispute, is a fraction of the cost of litigation.

- Disputes involve emotions which must be dealt with before a resolution will feel satisfying. You are the best one to express your own feelings.

- You know exactly what the dispute is about, and what you need to resolve it.

- You are better able to devise creative solutions to meet your needs than anyone else. Mediation allows for a fresh approach which assists you in reviewing alternatives and focusing on your priorities and objectives.

- If mediation fails, you are still free to use other methods of ADR or the courts. Even unsuccessful mediation is not a waste. The process serves to narrow and clarify the issues and will often settle money issues. Mediation also allows for an early exchange of information and removes much of the misunderstanding and false assumptions which preclude early settlement, often paving the way to later agreement.

I offer some additional benefits of mediation from my own experience:

- Mediation provides an opportunity to all concerned to review the "facts of life" face to face with your opponent and not filtered through counsel who might lose some of the flavour in the translation or soften the content in an effort to spare your sensibilities. Litigation encourages both sides to look at the case in its most optimistic light. You expect your lawyer to dwell on the strong points of the case. Some lawyers overemphasize the strengths so much that they fail to discuss the risks and problems that every case possesses. In one case, for example, the lawyer declared during the course of the mediation, "We can't lose this case." This presented his opponent the opportunity to point out seven ways the case would be lost. This had a sobering and salutary effect on the negotiation, prompting the overly optimistic lawyer's client to take the settlement proposal more seriously.

- You speak directly to each other, clarifying misunderstandings, rather than allowing them to fester and grow.

- You are able to unburden yourself of emotions which often drive disputes in a safe and constructive way, with the assistance of the mediator.

- When agreement is reached, it directly responds to the needs of each party. You, the parties, are not limited by the jurisdictional or other constraints imposed on judges or the imagination of arbitrators, judges, or ex-judges, who are not familiar with your needs. You are only constrained by the limits of your imagination and creativity.

- Through mediation, the amount of employee time and money consumed in a dispute is controlled. More party involvement results in a tighter reign on counsel, costs, and the manner in which the case is conducted.

- For multiparty, multiissue disputes that are often too cumbersome for the courts, mediation, as a flexible process, has the effect of narrowing the issues and focusing parties on their respective interests. No rules govern who should be at the table or any other aspect of the process unless they make sense and are agreed to by the participants.

THE DECISION TO MEDIATE

Mediation is either agreed to by the parties and their counsel or, as is increasingly common, it is required by legislation or court direction as a first step before proceeding with conventional litigation. Many sophisticated litigants such as insurance companies, banks, governments, and large corporations require that all these cases be mediated unless it can be demonstrated that for policy, precedental or other cogent reasons mediation is not appropriate. In jurisdictions where mediation is mandatory in the absence of an exemption, all cases will be mediated. In Ontario, construction liens, family, and small claims court cases only, will be exempted.

Notwithstanding the exemption of family cases, there is a long tradition of mediating such cases. In extreme cases of power imbalance or physical abuse, mediation of family cases may not be appropriate. But, more often than not these days, the parties are demanding that their lawyers attempt mediation as a first step. This trend will continue as more people become aware that mediation is a powerful, viable, and highly successful option to litigation. Lawyers have noticed this shift in consumer attitudes and are quickly becoming staunch proponents of the process. Those who have done so reportedly are enjoying extremely busy practices.

GETTING THE OTHER SIDE TO COME TO THE TABLE

Once you have decided with your lawyer that you would prefer to mediate rather than litigate, how exactly do you go about getting the other party in the dispute to come to the mediation table? After all, there are at least two of you involved in the dispute and you can't have a mediation without the other party's consent unless the mediation is court mandated. There are several ways to broach the subject.

Direct Approach

More and more parties and lawyers are comfortable proposing mediation. They no longer see making the proposal as a sign of weakness. This change in attitude owes much to the growing recognition by most lawyers that their clients want to resolve their disputes quickly and inexpensively. The growth in demand for and legitimacy of mediation is every bit as important. You are demanding mediation of your disputes as knowledge of the process widens. Because winning and losing are no longer central to negotiations, thinking in terms of strength or weakness is similarly of less concern. So if you take the direct approach and ask the disputing party to mediate, chances are they will agree.

Indirect Approach

If there is a concern about the direct approach, an intermediary may be used. ADR providers are accustomed to proposing mediation and making it seem more like their idea than one of the party's.

Government Mandates

More and more governments are recognizing the benefits of mediation. Mandatory mediation is now required in Ontario for all civil non-family cases. Several other governments are considering implementing a programme of mandatory mediation based on the success of the Ontario Pilot Project.

Other Inducements

As an inducement to mediate, many insurance companies and others who have come to recognize its benefits, now offer to pay the mediator's fees, if the mediation is unsuccessful.

SHOULD I MEDIATE?—ESSENTIAL ELEMENTS

Rather than merely describing mediation and leaving it to others to decide whether it may or may not be appropriate, let us examine the esssential elements required for successful mediation.

Intent to Negotiate in Good Faith

First, all participants must intend to negotiate in good faith. You should be prepared to participate actively and completely in the process. That does not mean that there must be commitment to come to an agreement at all costs or that you must agree to compromise your essential interests. Rather, you should possess an optimistic state of mind and be ready to give it the "old college try."

Deciding whether you have the necessary motivation and desire requires introspection. If the dispute is so deeply entrenched that your emotional and financial commitment to pursuing it outweighs practical considerations for resolving the matter on a reasonable basis early, the chances of success are minimal.

There are many practical reasons for coming to early agreement such as cost savings, customer satisfaction, effective use of corporate resources, reduced stress, and the future relations between the disputants. We now live in a very small world where relationships are even more important.

Authority

If the mediation is to succeed, you must have full and flexible authority to enter into an agreement. Insufficient authority, particularly if this fact is undisclosed, will lead to failure. Having to make a telephone call to someone who has not been present during the negotiation guarantees difficulties.

Relationships—Is the Relationship Worth Preserving?

Another characteristic of successful mediations relates to the importance of the relationship between the parties and whether the relationship is worth preserving. It is arguable that most relationships are worth preserving on the theory that "what goes around comes around" in an ever-shrinking world. If mediation reduces the number of people bad-mouthing the company or industry, the effort may be well justified. Similarly, family relationships involved in inheritance or family disputes should be considered. It should be remembered that these disputes often affect several generations. Mediation is non-confrontational and cooperative. While litigation often leaves relationships in tatters, mediation often actually enhances them.

Flexibility

Critical to successful mediation is flexibility. The degree of flexibility is a good measure of a party's intent to negotiate in good faith. To succeed in mediation, the negotiation must be approached with an open mind. You should be prepared to listen carefully to the other party's perception of the dispute with a view to attempting to accommodate their legitimate needs without compromising your own. You also need to define your own needs and anticipate theirs. Because you will not be able to do this with 100% accuracy, you must be flexible.

Having examined your own intent, you should also examine the other party's intention to determine if insurmountable barriers will sabotage mediation. These barriers are discussed in Chapter 5.

WHEN IS THE BEST TIME TO MEDIATE?

The earlier in the process of trying to resolve the dispute you decide to use mediation, the less costly it will be, both financially and emotionally. Clearly, mediating before litigation has been started would be ideal, before attitudes have hardened and the adversarial system has worked its magic. If you are at the critical stage in a dispute of having to decide whether to commence litigation or mediate, the answer should be clear by now. Mediate first.

The Role of the Lawyer

In Chapter 4 the lawyer's role is examined at length. It may be useful here to discuss the role of lawyers in mediations which occur not as part of the litigation process but because the parties are seeking to avoid a lawsuit. For example, you and your business partner or wife are considering breaking up the business or marriage, your insurance company is resisting paying a claim, or you are having a fight with a supplier over defective parts.

Where the issues in dispute have a significant legal component, it goes without saying that legal advice should be obtained before negotiations commence. Parties in dispute generally usually negotiate before taking any further steps. The critical point is what should happen if the negotiations break down. Do you charge off and start the lawsuit or pause to reflect upon whether, with some assistance, the negotiation might continue? This is the seminal point when you may decide to mediate before launching the lawsuit.

The question is, should you involve your lawyer? Certainly your lawyer will be of great assistance to you as a consultant, before mediation, helping you develop your negotiation strategy, assisting you to understand your chances in a lawsuit in court and your other alternatives. In addition, your lawyer can help you select an appropriate mediator. But should your lawyer accompany you to the mediation? Often this question may be answered for you by your opponent who may insist on having her lawyer present. If this is the case, then you should, as a general rule, have yours along as well.

If the matter is complex and you have confidence that your lawyer will add value because he possesses strong negotiation skills as well as the ability to assist you with legal advice, reality checks and emotional support, you will have a valuable mediation team member.

Last but far from least, expense must be considered. But if litigation can be averted by involving your lawyer in the mediation process, you have your answer. The mediator will be of assistance to you and your opponent in answering the question. It may be that the mediator suggests starting without lawyers, keeping open the option of involving them as needed.

TIP Not only will a knowledgeable lawyer help you with the legal analysis, reality checks, and negotiation, your lawyer can be a great source of needed support during the ups and downs that accompany difficult negotiations, providing you with objectivity, real emotional support, and good humour when the going gets tough.

The Stages of Litigation

One-on-one negotiations have failed. The parties have already appointed legal counsel. Counsel are unable to resolve the matter between themselves. In fact, the dispute will have probably escalated to a higher level. This is the usual scenario before much thought is given to mediation. This is particularly so in cases where litigation has been started without a serious effort at negotiation.

Stage One: The Pleadings—Statements of Claim and Defence

There are actually three levels or escalation points in litigation. Stage One is the exchange of pleadings where, as you recall, each side puts its case at its absolute and often exaggerated best in documents called The Statement of Claim and the Statement of Defence. Things are said in these documents which often produce incredible anger. For example, the pleadings often suggest that the plaintiff is malingering, lying, or attempting to defraud or extort money from the innocent defendant. The defendant might deny all responsibility. There are also sharp disagreements over the amount of damage which ought to be paid to either party. The defendant might file a counter-claim for damages suffered as a result of actions taken by the plaintiff.

Stage Two: Discoveries—The Emotional Investment

A second level of entrenchment results after discoveries are held. Discoveries, to reiterate, are the informal method in litigation by which information is exchanged and tested for relevancy and veracity. During the oral discovery, the plaintiff is cross-examined at great length by defendant's counsel in the hope of finding support for and confirming the allegations in the pleadings. The defendant is similarly cross-examined. There is nothing wrong, per se, with this quest for information in a lawsuit. In fact, it is very important. It does not seem to matter how counsel approach the process. Whether counsel are clinical, dispassionate, logical and precise, or hostile, pushy, aggressive, and arrogant, the result of having gone through the discovery process is usually the same. The plaintiff sees only that the claim is being denied and steps are being taken to avoid dealing with the claim. The defendant feels wronged, indignant, and more determined than ever to resist the claim.

Stage Three: Discoveries—The Financial Investment

Stage Three is the amount of financial investment in the case. Apart from trial, discoveries are by far the most expensive part of the litigation process because they often last for days. Usually discoveries are postponed until all the evidence is collected and sifted. All witnesses will be interviewed and statements recorded. If there are experts, their reports will often be obtained after discoveries because the transcripts of the discovery will be compared to all of the foregoing for inconsistencies in order to achieve an advantage at trial or to impugn the credibility of the parties in the hope of making their side more credible. Discoveries are not simply an information-assembling and -dissemination exercise. They are carefully prepared for and orchestrated as part of a win/lose process.

::::::

It is precisely because of these stages of entrenchment and escalation that mediation works best when these levels are minimized or avoided altogether. In order to maximize the benefits of mediation, it is necessary to begin at the earliest possible moment. This requires some deliberation in light of the view among some lawyers that mediation should always occur after the discovery process. I do not agree. The question that must be posed at this point is: are the costs, time, and likely negative impact of discoveries likely to yield benefits greater than an early mediation? It may be that efforts to obtain needed information may have to occur before the question can be answered. Clearly if there is a lack of cooperation or information is being withheld, it will be easy to answer the question in the affirmative. It may also depend on what is at stake.

If the mediation does not succeed, your options are still open to proceed with discovery. I have also been in mediations where it became evident that discovery would be useful on one or two points. The mediation was then adjourned until discoveries were completed.

Discovery is a process which assumes reluctance to share information. It can be very antagonistic; in fact, it presupposes suppression of relevant material, not cooperation. The process itself has a negative effect on the parties' attitudes to settlement. A successful mediation requires that both sides have access to, and share, all critical information and data needed by each other to answer, in their own way, the question, "Are we better off, all things considered, entering into this agreement today or are we better off not doing so and holding out for a better deal or going to court and taking our chances with a win/lose outcome?" This is a question for the client to answer with input from counsel based on the information needs of the particular dispute.

Most disputes are simple one- or two-issue cases complicated by emotional overlays or factual misunderstandings. If you are prepared to share your information and your opponent is of the same view, discovery will not be necessary. Since having discovery at a later date is still an option, nothing is lost by trying the more cooperative approach. If it emerges during the mediation that information has been withheld intentionally, obviously the withholding party's intention to negotiate in good faith has to be re-evaluated. In most cases there is no advantage whatsoever in withholding information. Doing so will harden the attitude of your opponent who has every right to compel the production of the information if it is relevant in the litigation process.

Because winning or losing in court is the focus of the adversarial system, counsel, of course, want to engage in extensive discovery. But if resolving the dispute is the objective and getting the information necessary to making intelligent decisions concerning appropriate options, the main concern, the parties can agree to share what is important and rely only upon the agreed shared material in the negotiations.

Some will say it's naive to believe that crucial information will be shared openly. Obviously, there are cases where there is good reason to doubt the good faith or intentions of your opponent. Usually the process of preparation for mediation and premediation exchange of information will reveal such intentions. Until you have tangible proof that information is not going to be forthcoming, giving your opponent the benefit of the doubt may well be in your very best interest. Remember, you must always weigh the negative effect of discovery and its cost against your objective, which is early resolution on a basis that is agreeable to *you*. Remember also, mediation is voluntary. If during the course of the mediation it becomes obvious that your opponent is a selective and imperfect historian, you have the option to end the mediation if the situation is not corrected.

Possible Outcome Of Trial and its Influence on Mediation

Outcome at trial is a very important consideration in deciding whether or not to mediate. Your lawyer's considered opinion of the chances of winning or losing in court forms a backdrop to your preparation for mediation. It has a lot to do with formulating your walk-away position. Having a clear understanding of your chances of winning or losing at trial is important, but it is not the only factor to be weighed carefully in the balance.

Other factors must be considered. In any dispute, certain things are known which influence the decision to avoid a win/lose outcome at trial:

- The other side thinks enough of their case to proceed and so far have not caved in to your demands. Only one of you can win.

- The costs of the process. If your opponent doesn't fully appreciate or has not been properly advised of the potential costs of litigation, mediation is an excellent opportunity to make this point.

- Losing is always a possibility. No lawyer that I know will guarantee success. Even the most aggressive will concede "there is always a chance of losing." In fact, the better lawyers only win a little over 50% of their cases. This is because in most cases the lawyers are evenly matched. Also like a jockey, the lawyer has to ride the horse he draws; he can't change the facts or the law.

- War has consequences; chief among them is stress and ruined relationships. The annals of litigation are rife with stories of bittersweet or hollow victory.

WHEN TO AVOID MEDIATION

Too often, the decision not to mediate is made for the wrong reasons. Individuals who are unfamiliar with the process or persons whose interests may not be well served by the decision to mediate, block the process. A question I ask is, "Will the parties be worse off for trying to mediate this dispute or not?" If you have very little to lose and much to gain, it's worth a try.

However, not all disputes benefit from mediation. Certain cases involving physical or sexual abuse or harassment in the workplace may be inappropriate for mediation. Occasionally it may be seen as strategically useful to send a warning to competitors. Cases involving fraud, which a company or industry will not tolerate, may also fall into this category. The decision to mediate must be made intelligently after reviewing a number of factors. For example, if a company's investigation reveals that a claim is being advanced fraudulently, the company might use the mediation to put its position forward together with its evidence of fraud and its corporate policy that, under no circumstances will such claims be paid. Such a company should approach the mediation with an open mind and be prepared, if an appropriate explanation is advanced, to change it. In one such mediation the claimant saw fit to withdraw his claim and everyone was ahead of the game.

Mediation may also be inappropriate where a party is seeking public recognition of a right, particularly if the need is for the application of the court's discretion to award punitive damages. Examples might include cases of racial or gender discrimination, sexual harassment, and wrongful termination where the employer's conduct was abusive or deceitful. As a general rule of thumb, where the parties are by reason of strong emotions—for example, some victims of physical, mental, or sexual abuse—incapable of communicating directly with one another, the chances of a successful mediation are reduced. Similarly, cases involving dishonesty on the part of one of the parties such as forgery, theft of property, or cases of intentionally inflicted harm will have less chance of success.

If there is a real concern that the parties may end up further apart or concerns that an injustice will be perpetuated, mediation may be inappropriate. However, outright contra-indications to mediation are very different from what is described in Chapter 5 as barriers to successful mediation. Properly handled, barriers are usually easily overcome.

Witheld Information

Blindly agreeing to mediate a dispute when information critical to properly evaluating your opponent's case hasn't been shared or developed will produce failure because the parties will resist, and so they should, making uninformed decisions. To do otherwise would be to buy a pig in a poke. Failure to obtain and share necessary expert or medical reports are typical examples. The parties will not have enough information to weigh resolution options intelligently in order to decide if their essential interests are better served by agreement or by pursuing alternatives such as a lawsuit

Mediation, however, may well serve a beneficial purpose in assisting the parties to proceed more harmoniously towards the point where intelligent decisions can be made, even if the decision is to pursue a lawsuit. Problems are encountered when parties unrealistically expect mediation to produce an immediate result, despite the lack of information. This is more in the realm of magic than mediation.

The Single-Issue Dispute: All or Nothing

Where the dispute is only about one thing such as who gets the inheritance or whether the unsecured creditors are out of luck, the decision to mediate may be based solely on how much is at stake. Two types of situations occur: the jackpot mentality or the nothing-to-lose scenario.

The bonanza syndrome or jackpot mentality occurs when parties are locked in a battle where *to them* the stakes are so high they would risk losing to win the prize. The prize can be anything from money, winning, vindication, setting an important precedent, humiliating their opponent, or teaching them a lesson.

When corporate egos do battle, a variation on the theme is evident. Winning at all costs may not be in the interests of the company or its shareholders but where management is unchecked, this may occur.

Where both parties are propelled by aggressive legal opinions concerning their respective chances of winning the litigation, where their resources are equally matched, where their future relationship is apparently unimportant and where the stakes are very high, this phenomenon may also be observed.

The flip side of the jackpot mentality is the nothing-to-lose scenario. Here, a disputant may be facing bankruptcy, annihilation, and oblivion. There may be no options available to them apart from a complete victory in court on a technicality. Rolling the dice may be the last hope of a desperate opponent who wants to delay the inevitable in the hope of a miracle. In these cases, a court administered *coup de grace* may be the only realistic way to resolve the dispute.

The mentality that best describes this phenomenon is the story of Ali, the camel driver, who, when summoned before the caliph for stealing, promised that he would make the caliph's camel speak within two years if he would only spare Ali's miserable life. Ali's wife later chided him for his foolish promise. Ali replied that a lot can happen in two years:

- The caliph might die;
- The camel might die;
- Ali might die; or
- The camel might learn to speak.

ARBITRATION—AN ALTERNATIVE OR SUPPLEMENT TO MEDIATION

For mediation to be an attractive process, all parties must perceive that any likely agreement will satisfy their essential interests to a greater extent than other readily available alternatives. However, if after completing your analysis there are unequivocal signs that mediation will not work, other forms of ADR should be considered. Arbitration may be the ADR answer if mediation has not done the job or is seen as not being up to the job. The problem with arbitration and other forms of adjudicative or top-down, decision-imposed ADR is that they have the tendency over time to mutate into something that looks more and more like litigation, with protracted discoveries, procedural wrangling, and endless cavalcades of experts and other witnesses. The parties to the dispute lose control over the process.

What is Arbitration?

Parties in conflict privately select a neutral third party to decide the matter for them. After hearing the parties and other witnesses' evidence and their lawyers, the arbitrator renders an award, usually in writing, in favour of one or the other. The award may or may not be binding depending on the terms of reference given to the arbitrator.

Mediation and arbitration have common attributes such as the choice of a neutral decision maker, privacy and confidentiality, speed and lower expense than litigation and, perhaps most important, the ability to tailor the process to fit the needs of the parties and the dispute.

Mediation vs. Arbitration

There are some clear and some subtle differences to be aware of when deciding whether to mediate or arbitrate. For a detailed comparison of these processes see the table at the end of the chapter.

MEDIATION/ARBITRATION (MED-ARB)

This is an ADR process in which the parties agree that the mediation, if unsuccessful, will turn into an arbitration with the mediator performing the function of arbitrator.

This hybrid process is becoming more and more popular because it purports to combine the best features of both mediation and arbitration. It is appropriate when the parties have sufficient faith in the neutral's expertise and where the neutral indeed possesses expertise. This point requires special emphasis if the parties are not represented by legal counsel and the subject matter of the dispute is complex and fraught with potential problems for the unwary decision maker.

Med-Arb sets up an interesting dynamic. Either the parties will work hard to come to agreement to avoid the possibility of an unfavourable result, or the party who thinks he holds all the cards will not engage enthusiastically in the mediation process, being confident of victory in the arbitration phase.

What is predictable is the behaviour of parties who realize that, in the event of impasse, the mediator will call the shot. The parties will "pitch" the mediator or attempt to curry favour with him. They may also not be as forthcoming or open in the mediation phase, attempting to mask their blemishes for fear of adversely affecting the outcome in the arbitration phase. Correspondingly, there will be heightened emphasis on the other side's blemishes which could degenerate into an undesirable positional, highly argumentative, and less interest-based problem-solving climate during the mediation phase.

The Med-Arb model will suit some disputes quite well, particularly those with few emotional undercurrents where the parties have genuine and well-founded differences and a very high degree of trust in the expertise of the mediator. An example would be an international contracts dispute which concerns whether a certain practice was "standard" in the industry.

An Alternative

If the mediation is deadlocked at the end over one issue (the others having been resolved and various impasse strategies having failed), the parties may ask the mediator to provide an advisory opinion on the issue that is preventing agreement. This approach may well satisfy all concerned assuming they have faith in the mediator's opinion and the mediator is agreeable. I would suggest this option be considered only in rare cases where the mediator has unquestioned credentials and only after all else has failed.

Construction cases may be better suited to Med-Arb than most disputes. They tend to involve highly technical issues and complex contracts. Industry practice is often an issue and the parties are often bitterly divided. Who is "at fault" seems very important to the parties in some construction cases, not surprisingly because reputations are often involved.

	MEDIATION	ARBITRATION
Process	Informal, designed by the parties. Focuses on interest, not positions or who is right or wrong.	More formal, rights based, asks who is right and who is wrong. There is a winner and a loser. Designed by the parties.
Control	Parties control process and result.	Parties control process but not the result.
Agreement	Never binding until parties are in agreement.	Decision usually binding when rendered by the arbitrator, but may not be.
Knowledge	Mediator has basic knowledge of field, expertise usually left to the experts representing the parties.	Arbitrator is expected to be an expert. May have to choose between two or more experts' opinions when rendering the award.
Tone	Collaborative, problem solving, less likely to be hostile or negative.	Competitive, winner takes all. Formal, unaccommodating.
Cost	Less	More
Stakes	Low. Nothing to lose except the effort to resolve. Usually narrows the issues and can promote understanding. Failure should only result if other options are more attractive than the proposals on the table. The cost is usually much lower than any other alternative.	High. One party wins, the other loses. The cost of arbitration is usually much higher than mediation.
Time	Shorter—Allows parties to get on with their lives.	Longer—due to formality of procedures.
Third Party Neutral	Chosen more for skills as a professional negotiator of unquestioned neutrality. Chosen for ability to design and conduct a process that will likely produce agreement and permit all stakeholders to be heard.	An expert in the field respected by both parties. Particularly useful when there are complex technical issues.
Bias	Mediator's views less important, therefore fear of bias is lessened.	Bias a real concern. Use of three arbitrators may ensure each side a voice at the decision-making table usually with a neutral chairman to decide between them. Will be more costly, however.
Party Participation	Much higher. Parties negotiate directly with assistance from the mediator, counsel, and experts.	Much lower. Parties state position directly or through counsel and experts. Have no control over the result.
Closure	Not guaranteed but likely to be more acceptable to both parties if achieved.	Guaranteed but only one party will be victorious.

3

THE MEDIATION PROCESS

A Step-By-Step Look at a Typical Mediation

To realize the full potential of mediation, the process needs to be thoroughly understood. Much has been written about it, but usually by mediators for mediators. As a result, a tremendous amount of jargon has already crept into this young profession! Some writings suggest dark doings, mysterious rites, and voodoo-like rituals. The process of mediation is really very uncomplicated.

Looking at the negotiation through the mediator's eyes may bring further clarity and understanding and thereby improve your chances of successful mediation. I see the process as passing through five main stages (see Mediation Process Checklist at the end of this chapter) which are achieved in progression. There are no time limits, and they tend to be seamless, one leading fluidly to another as the mediation unfolds.

The mediation may founder on the rocks during any stage for a number of the reasons described in Chapter 5 as barriers. With hard work by the parties and the mediator, the mediation may be refloated and find its way into the safe harbour of agreement. Depending on the dispute, complexity, number of parties, their level of preparation, and degree of commitment to the process, a mediation may take anywhere from one session of three to five hours to several sessions.

STAGE ONE—THE CONVENING STAGE

Before any mediation session occurs, a lot of work has to be done. Don't expect the unexpected. Speak to the mediator beforehand, if possible. Understand how that particular mediator likes to work. Remember that although the mediator may be in charge of the process during the mediation, the mediator does not own it. If something about the design needs improvement, the mediator should be open to suggestions. Perhaps the parties are not comfortable with one another in the same room. Some work initially may be needed to assist them to communicate directly. This should be brought to the attention of the mediator. In more complex cases, the parties should work closely with the mediator to design a process that has the best chance of meeting their objectives. For example, it might be appropriate to organize a separate meeting of conflicting experts in the hope of narrowing or eliminating their differences.

The Agreement to Mediate

Before any step is taken in the mediation itself, an Agreement to Mediate should be signed by the parties and the mediator. (A sample agreement appears in Appendix B). The agreement should outline the commitment of both parties to the process and spell out the obligations of each between themselves and with the mediator. A good agreement will cover the parties' desire and commitment to mediate. It will also describe the process as:

- a cooperative method of negotiation with the goal of a consensual outcome based on mutual understanding;
- requiring open and honest communication and that full disclosure is expected;
- a voluntary one which may be terminated at any time by either of the parties or the mediator;
- one where the parties determine how the mediation will conclude;
- confidential whereby the parties and the mediator respect this confidentiality except where it has been otherwise agreed upon.

    The agreement should also include:

- The role of the mediator as an impartial neutral party with no interest in the outcome of the dispute. The mediator must not have had a previous relationship with either party. The mediator will not offer legal advice but will make appropriate suggestions to assist in the negotiations.
- The mediator cannot be called as a witness, nor can her notes be used in legal proceedings.

- The parties will be represented by counsel. If they are not, then they will obtain legal advice as needed and any mediated agreement will be vetted by the parties' respective counsel.
- A brief description of the dispute.
- The name of the mediator, date, time, and location, and a deadline for concluding the mediation.
- Materials to be provided to the mediator and the required date.
- The mediator's fee, other costs, overtime and cancellation fees, and the date by which notification must be made.
- The mediator's fee will be paid by the parties equally or as otherwise agreed.
- A provision indemnifying the mediator from claims that may arise, for example, if one party reneges on the agreement.
- Names of those who will attend and a statement that they will be present at the mediation. In the case of a corporate party, this should be someone with full authority to enter into an agreement. Typically, the parties and their lawyers will attend.
- Provision for third parties, other than the disputing parties, to participate only if the parties and mediator consent.

Typically, the mediator will supply the draft agreement to mediate. You should read it carefully and be sure you fully understand all the terms. If you and your lawyer want changes, these matters should be discussed at an early stage with the mediator and the other party.

Location

The location should be on neutral territory, informal and businesslike, with access to rooms for private discussions and phone calls. Hotels, Special Examiner's offices, Court House facilities, or even one of the lawyer's boardrooms (provided you are comfortable with the arrangement) are some of the usual places to hold mediations.

How Long Should the Mediation Last?

Sessions should be tailored to the dispute, remembering that human beings are rarely productive in intensive, often emotional and stressful conditions for more than four or five hours. Agree in advance on time frames. Don't assume that an hour or two is enough unless you are very close to agreement. A good rule of thumb would be that if agreement has been reached on all issues save one or two and the tenor of the discussions is cooperative, you are close. After four or five hours, agree to another session unless so little has been accomplished that another session would be futile.

I have seen amazing results at second sessions when the parties agreed to return on specific terms—for example, a mortgage dispute involving complicated renewals, interest rate adjustments, and something called the "deemed reinvestment principle." The parties agreed to put their accountants together and, if they made no progress, they would select a neutral accountant who would act as an advisor to the mediator. The accountants continued at loggerheads (because they had a vested interest in being right). The neutral accountant was brought in and prepared a report which was used by the parties to conclude the matter at a second mediation session.

STAGE TWO—INTRODUCTIONS AND GROUND RULES

The mediator takes the lead by introducing himself, making a brief reference to his credentials, and then introducing the parties or allowing them to introduce themselves. Establishing an informal, comfortable climate initially is very important. He may invite people to take off their jackets and make themselves comfortable, understanding there is usually a lot of tension and apprehension being experienced around the table.

Time will be spent describing the process as a hopeful and successful means of achieving resolution. I explain my role as that of assisting the parties to achieve their own agreement and emphasize the voluntary and confidential aspects of mediation.

Ground rules, about courtesy, communication, time constraints, interruptions, and items relating to personal comfort, are all canvassed. How private meetings will be conducted, the order of proceeding, as well as each party's intention to negotiate in good faith and their level of authority are

---

TIP   Arrive early to meet with your team and deal with any last-minute items. Being late puts you in the position of offering apologies and explanations—not a great beginning. Establish a cordial businesslike atmosphere by shaking hands with everyone and making sure you learn everyone's name and position.

Be yourself. Don't be overly deferential to the mediator or, as I have seen, try to prove that you enjoy a close personal relationship. Setting a friendly tone says that you are comfortable both with your position and the process. This will help put your opponents at ease. Be friendly but don't go too far. Joking around and making inappropriate remarks sends a different, negative message both to your opponents and the mediator.

reviewed. Some time will be spent on the order of proceeding as well as practical things such as physical needs, making sure everyone knows they are free to take a break to speak to their lawyer, make a phone call or use the facilities.

The mediator may well want everyone to discuss their intentions and authority levels at the outset. This will not only ensure there are no problems but will also get everyone's commitment to the process on the table.

Intention

Two factors are critical for a successful mediation. The first is the *intention* to negotiate in *good faith*. You do not need an intention to settle at all costs. Quite the contrary—you must always have your own best interests at heart. You should approach the process, hopeful that a resolution will be achieved, but not with blind faith.

You should have some settlement scenarios in mind that will work for you. You must be prepared to listen carefully to the other side's point of view and to modify your approach as new information comes to light or ideas are developed. Without flexibility and an open mind, very little will be possible. Negotiation is not about capitulation. It's about coming to an agreement that works for everyone. Any proposed agreement must be perceived by the participants as better than their other alternatives.

Authority

The second vital factor for success in mediation is authority. You as an individual party or any corporate representative should have the authority to resolve the dispute. There must be flexibility since only in the simplest negotiation is it possible to anticipate everything. If you have limited authority, this must be disclosed at the beginning of the mediation. For example, if you are only authorized (as I have heard) "to listen with an open mind," you had better say so pretty early or face the accusation later that you were not negotiating in good faith.

When the mediator is finished, he or she will ask if there are any questions or comments. Even if the invitation is not extended, this is the time to obtain clarification on any point you may think is important. This is also the time to clarify questions about limits of authority or other process concerns. For example, "John, excuse me, you spoke of limited authority. I would like to know more about that." It may be that John has only been authorized to simply repeat an offer previously rejected, in which case you might decide to terminate the mediation or John might have to obtain ratification of any agreement by his board of directors or president. This might or might not be acceptable to you.

Goals

The mediator will usually confirm his understanding of what the parties would like to accomplish. In my experience, what works best is if the parties, with the assistance of their lawyers, explain how they see the dispute from their perspective. I urge them to put all their cards on the table. The mediator will say something to the effect that the hard work of negotiation is making absolutely sure your opponents understand each and every factor they must weigh in the balance when making the critical decision at the end of the process. The decision that must be made is whether or not to leave the process without agreement, or to resolve the dispute on whatever basis is developed during the negotiation. A common example is whether to accept the insurance company's offer of compensation or attempt to improve on it by proceeding with litigation.

TIP During this phase resist the temptation to (1) talk to your neighbour; (2) flip through your file; (3) twirl your pen; (4) look out the window; (5) interrupt with questions or points of order or other matters that may occur to you. This type of behaviour will be interpreted as nervousness or disrespect, neither of which will benefit your cause or send a positive message to the other side. Your body language and tone of voice also send a message whether or not you are at ease with your position and the process.

Participation

It is critical for the parties, as well as for counsel, to engage in the mediation process. You should ensure that you have what you need to make notes. This leads me to a most important point. When somebody is speaking, they should not be interrupted. This is important for two reasons. First, everyone at the table is entitled to courtesy. Interrupting may be misconstrued as rudeness. Second, it is difficult to listen carefully if you are trying to make your own point.

> **TIP** Try to appear engaged and address your remarks directly to your opponents, *not the mediator*, making as much eye contact as possible. You are not trying to persuade the mediator, because she will not judge or say who is right or wrong. You should address yourself to your opponents, sending the message that you intend to work with them to resolve the matter in a mutually satisfactory way.

STAGE THREE—INFORMATION EXCHANGE AND ISSUE IDENTIFICATION

The first part of Stage Three consists of the opening statements where each party puts forward its version of the dispute. This is the time for a clear, concise rendition of the story from each party's perspective. It should flow as smoothly and unprovocatively as possible and take no more time than is necessary to cover the key points. That will be anywhere from ten to twenty minutes unless the matter is extraordinarily complex.

While this first round is progressing, the mediator will pay a lot of attention to the speaker and the listeners' reactions to the speaker, making notes of observations and suspected key interests.

The object of this stage is to make sure that each party understands the other's point of view thoroughly and objectively. Interventions by the mediator will be infrequent and directed primarily to assisting in clarifying and summarizing what has been said.

Watch, Listen, and Learn

The importance of listening very carefully to what is being said cannot be overemphasized. After all, half of negotiation is listening. Make notes but pay close attention to things like tone, attitude, body language, and what is not said. If anything is unclear, make a note to ask a neutrally framed question.

TIP Careful listening is even more important than speaking. By observing closely things such as pitch, tone, and body language, you will receive helpful clues to your opponent's key concerns. You are also demonstrating respect, which will be appreciated and enhance the chances of success.

Make detailed notes. You will undoubtedly hear many things you disagree with, or would like to comment upon. I divide the page into two parts. On the right, I note the sense of what is being said. On the left, I note my observations, questions, and key points.

Opening Statements: You Are Up

If you are up first, proceed in the order you have agreed with your team. Your team might be only you or you and your lawyer. In more complex cases, there might also be an accountant, engineer, or perhaps two or three business partners. In rare cases there may be more than one lawyer with different specialities. Typically a corporate team will consist of an appropriate company representative and a lawyer. In individual disputes the team is usually the individual and his lawyer.

As discussed in Chapter 5 under "Lack of Preparation," you will have developed an approach to the mediation. Each of you will have assignments or if you are on your own, you will be wearing different hats and perform as a one-person band. Regardless, you will be following a well-prepared game plan. Perhaps the lawyer will summarize what the dispute is all about and why you had to commence the legal proceedings. State the issues from your perspective and your general approach to the dispute, as well as your preferred outcome.

It is important during your presentation to send some clear signals that you are there to get something accomplished and don't expect the other side to capitulate entirely to the blinding logic of your position. On the other hand, opening statements should state your position at its best and be made to sound as compelling as possible without being exaggerated. Blaming, accusing, and inflammatory or insulting language should be avoided at all costs. There are other ways to convey the impression that you are serious about pursuing your claim to an appropriate resolution.

Everyone on your team should have an assignment during this phase. Your lawyer might summarize the case if you are the claimant giving the reasons why the defendant is at fault, referring briefly to the medical reports and the consequences of the car accident, as well as the costs of continuing care and income loss, as well as general loss of enjoyment of life. You might speak to the impact of the accident on your life, career, and family, outlining the things you enjoyed but are no longer able to do. This says you are a well-prepared and organized team. You should also anticipate and deal with what will be said by your opponents.

While your team is presenting, do not interrupt them even if someone leaves out a key point; make a note of it and supplement what has been said when he or she is finished. You will only throw them off stride by interrupting and diminish the effect of their presentation.

If someone on the other side interrupts you, play it by ear. The mediator will usually not allow any interruptions, but if she does, you have a range of responses. If you perceive they are attempting to throw you off balance, simply ask them to stop and say that you will respond to questions at the appropriate time. The mediator will usually suggest that questions be held until everyone has had a chance to complete their opening statements, so that the process does not get sidetracked.

The mediator may ask questions and summarize in order to clarify what has been said. Generally the mediator will not ask difficult questions, rather questions calculated to ensure that your points have been clearly made. If the mediator asks questions which you consider unfair, you can defer to your lawyer or skate around them. The mediator's only interest should be to assist you to fully express your point of view.

Opening Statements: They Are Up

When it's their turn to speak, adopting a posture that is engaged, respectful, open, and interested will work well during this phase. Avoid negative behaviour such as looking at the ceiling, coughing or muttering, rolling your eyes, or turning your back to the speaker. Use common sense and common courtesy.

Clarification and Amplification

After the opening statements, everyone will be anxious to clarify, amplify, and rebut points. Hearing from everyone at the table again is very useful because it allows you to validate points that were made by your opponent which are inescapable or put a different spin on them. Do not ignore these points. Meet them and acknowledge their validity or, if possible, provide your own preferred spin. Likewise, answer questions that have been posed, even if the questions were rhetorical. Clarify anything that you remotely believe was not fully understood. "Jane, you said you find it inconceivable that any damage was done to my reputation by what you said. You should know that two days later several customers cancelled their orders with us."

Do not simply repeat your opening statement or position labouriously. Ask questions about points which have not been adequately answered. For example, "What I would still very much like to know is why the contractor proceeded to do the excavation work without a written order when, in all other instances during the construction, one was obtained?"

At the end of this round, all the key information needs of the parties should be met and no one should be saying, "Look, I still need to see an engineer's report proving the additional excavation was not contemplated in the original drawings." If fundamentally important information is missing, if it cannot be readily obtained, another session should be considered.

The mediator will then usually summarize the issues and discuss an agenda for the balance of the mediation. The main issues should be crystal clear at this point.

The Break

Breaks shouldn't be too long because the momentum of the process may falter. However, during the breaks, the parties are able to discuss among themselves their own performance and what they have heard. Also, a party may decide they require further information as a result of something they have heard. Maybe they will make a phone call or receive a fax.

Regrouping—What's Really Going On?

A break may be useful for a number of reasons:

- I like to reflect privately on what has unfolded for a few minutes, review my notes, and plan the best approach to continue. I then discuss my ideas with the parties.
- The parties will usually want to discuss what they have heard among themselves and modify their game plan accordingly.
- Physically, everyone needs to relax and recharge their batteries.
- Invariably, things may not have been said for fear of upsetting someone, derailing the process, or for strategic reasons. This is a useful time to discuss these matters privately with the mediator.

Private Meetings: Party-Mediator

The mediator will usually visit each party separately, explaining that whatever is revealed in such meetings will not be shared with the other side unless permission is given. It is important to build trust with all parties and have a free-flowing discussion about aspects of the case that might not have been revealed directly to the opponent up to this point.

This is the opportunity to disclose sensitive information to the mediator. It is a time for the mediator to probe and confirm matters which may only have been alluded to and to verify impressions which may or may not be correct. If done publicly, these might cause embarrassment. Thus, private meetings can be very valuable.

Experienced mediators develop an ability to grasp the underlying concerns which have not been expressed by either party. The private meeting is a safe opportunity to probe, amplify, or dispel any such concerns. Before I leave the meeting, I obtain permission to reveal anything I think will be useful in moving the process forward. Examples might be:

- The defendant is dying and returning to Asia. (If this is indeed true and the defendant has no assets in Canada, a judgement against her will be worthless.)

- The defendant is a nephew of one of the senior partners in the law firm representing him. (Legal costs will not be an important factor for him in this lawsuit.)

- The defendant is currently doing $2,000,000 worth of business with the plaintiff's subsidiary. (Suing someone who gives you a lot of business may not be in your best interests. You will want to preserve the relationship if possible.)

- The plaintiff has an opinion from an expert confirming gross negligence by the defendant's engineer. (Things are looking bleak if this goes to court unless the defendant has an equally pre-eminent expert's report in which case this should be tabled right away.)

- The defendant is in possession of a report from another insurance company confirming that the plaintiff's family made numerous similar claims in suspicious circumstances. (This claim may not be worth pursuing further unless a very good explanation is available, in which case it should be put forward right away to dispel the defendant's view that this is a fraudulent claim. Clearly this is a barrier to resolution which must be surmounted to resolve the dispute.)

It may be that if the mediator puts these facts forward privately, the affected party will be able to react without embarrassment. Floating various settlement options through the mediator may also be less risky. If they are rejected, the mediator will obtain helpful reasons why the alternative is a non-starter, and relay that information to the proponent, as well as take the heat for the proposal so that the proponent doesn't have to. The downside to acting as a go-between is that the message may lose something in the translation. The risks of this occurring have to be weighed in each case against the benefits.

I find that meeting with everyone privately, even if I'm asked not to reveal anything said to me in confidence, gives me a better idea of what the real issues and agendas are and provides clues about where the process has to go to achieve meaningful agreement.

After meeting with everyone, I should have a very clear understanding of what the dispute is really all about, and of the parties' needs, as well. The mediator will try to spend an equal amount of time with each party but don't be too concerned if this is not the case. The better working assumption is that there is a good reason for a lengthier meeting unrelated to favouritism.

Process Options After the Break: Remain Separated or Resume Joint Session?

After the break the mediator will then decide, with the help of the parties, which options to pursue. The optimum course should be clear after the private meetings with all parties are complete. It might be the case that critical information must be obtained in order to advance matters. For example, if the parties are stuck between diametrically opposed real estate appraisals or medical reports, it may be agreed to adjourn on certain terms to allow the experts to meet and clarify their submissions. A third appraiser might be called upon to decide the outstanding point.

Sometimes anger, betrayal, and resentment are the real driving forces behind a disagreement. For example, the plaintiff may feel badly treated by the defendant insurance company. The mediator may decide to reconvene to discuss these matters and to let the plaintiff express his/her feelings directly to the defendant. The family may have suffered a great deal. To deny these feelings and not discuss them is to invite failure. But dealing with them appropriately can be critical to early resolution.

It may be useful, as well, to get everyone together to recap the issues and identify what is important from each side's perspective, as well as to reconfirm everyone's resolve to work towards a solution.

Reconvening

A group brainstorming session can be an enormously creative and useful process in generating potential options for a settlement. Provided that emotional concerns have been resolved and dialogue between the parties is possible, all-party brainstorming ensures that no time is wasted exploring alternatives that one party cannot accept.

In some cases there may be multiple defendants or what are called third parties. A third party is a party added to the litigation by the defendant on the theory that "if I'm responsible, they have to cover my losses." When there are a number of defendants and third parties, it may be useful to convene a separate meeting among them, apart from the plaintiff, to provide them with an opportunity to discuss sharing responsibility and in what proportions. For example, Jane slips and falls in a large shopping centre. She sues the owner of the mall and the store operator where she fell. The store operator joins

XYZ Cleaning Co. Inc. as a third party because they were in the store that day doing the carpets. The mall, store operator, and XYZ have issues of responsibility to discuss among themselves that are of no interest to Jane. She is concerned about compensation and perhaps also about an assurance that this will never happen to anyone else.

Remaining Separate To Develop Common Ground

In less complex cases or highly charged, volatile situations, it may be appropriate to remain apart and develop options separately, using the mediator as a go-between. When doing so, review and revise your preparation material, your assumptions, and premediation options. The mediator may help with reality checks if your assumptions are too aggressive. More important, the mediator will remind you about the concerns and needs of your opponent. You will then be in a position to do a critical analysis, testing possible solutions against your walk-away position.

TIP Whether you reconvene or not, it is very important that periodically during the course of the mediation the parties convey messages with a hopeful tone, such as, "We are committed to this process and to achieving a result that will work for both of us," or "The best solution is the one that you and our people can both buy into." If you continue to reiterate your commitment and demonstrate flexibility, your counterparts should follow suit.

Stage three can take one to two hours or more, depending on the complexity of the case. Normally the nature of the problem to be resolved is apparent after one or two hours.

STAGE FOUR—PROBLEM SOLVING

If the result of the consultations in Stage Three is that everyone is in agreement on the definition of the problem and its components, it is time to go to Stage Four. At the beginning of Stage Four, the problem and its subcomponents are agreed to in joint session. In more complex cases, it may be useful to write out the issues. At this point it is necessary to strike an agenda and, with everyone's agreement, list the issues in the order the parties' wish them discussed. The mediator may make suggestions at an early stage, choosing less contentious issues with little or no chance of creating an impasse. It may also be worthwhile to review time constraints and agree on a realistic timetable for each issue.

Generating Options

A large part of Stage Four is generating options that might address the issues. Any number of techniques may be used depending on the climate, parties, and time constraints. Ideally, the parties will jointly brainstorm with the mediator pushing themselves creatively to search for options that encompass as many of the parties' respective interests as possible.

The final step in Stage Four is testing these options against reality and each party's alternatives or walk-away position. Stage Four is the time in the mediation when the mediator must really earn her keep: challenging the parties to create value and assisting in the process, ensuring that negative behaviour is minimized and perhaps most importantly, assisting each party, gently but firmly, to see their alternatives objectively as only a neutral person can.

It is at this stage that mediations may stall due to impasse if the parties are unable to see the benefit of proceeding to agreement because their walk-away position is more attractive than any of the options for agreement on the table.

Testing Alternatives Against Your Walk-Away Position

I sometimes find it useful to ask each party to reflect privately on all the factors that have been identified and ask them to devise options which they think may resolve the matter in a mutually satisfactory way. When this is done in private, no embarrassment or feeling of premature commitment results. Here the mediator is of the most assistance. Acting as an agent of reality, the mediator reminds each party of the other's needs and assists with helpful ideas, all in the safety of a private meeting.

In order to evaluate options, a careful analysis is required. This requires that each party acknowledge they may lose at trial. Their lawyer must assist by providing an assessment of the case for the client, acknowledging the possibility of losing as well as winning. While this assessment is not capable of mathematical certainty, a careful lawyer will have a pretty good idea of the chances of winning and losing and the important variables that will bear on determining the winner and loser.

Clients often don't want to hear about losing and are, in effect, willing co-conspirators with their lawyers in denying the possibility of losing. While this is not usually the case, I have been involved in several mediations where neither side would acknowledge the slightest risk of losing. This creates a surreal twilight zone where both parties are supremely confident in their walk-away positions. The problem is that one of them is going to be wrong. A common explanation for this phenomenon is that the information they are relying on has only been partially developed or they may be unaware of a key fact. An effective mediation will ensure that all relevant information is shared and remove the possibility of this occurring. To avoid this conundrum, parties should approach the mediation with an open mind and avoid overly aggressive views of their chances of success in court unless they are completely justified.

The Analysis

If the claim is about money among other things, the lawyers will concede that:

- The lawsuit from beginning to the end of a trial will cost each party somewhere between $20,000 to $40,000. Remember the average is $38,000.
- Legal costs are rarely totally recovered by the winner. Rather, an award of costs on a "party and party" basis of around 50% is normal in litigation. Perhaps even more to the point, costs awards are not always *collected* as we discussed in Chapter 2.

These assumptions set the stage for understanding that common ground may be found in the mediation, even if both sides are overly optimistic about winning at trial.

Let us take the simple case where the judge has no latitude in awarding damages, where it's all or nothing.

Case Study

Alice and Bob are in a dispute over ownership of a diamond worth $100,000 and the judge must decide who has the better claim. Alice says, based on her lawyer's advice, she has a 60% chance of winning; Bob also says that he has a 60% chance of winning. Alice and Bob therefore both concede they have a 40% chance of losing.

Assume that legal fees for both will be $20,000 and that the winner will recover 50% of his/her costs. The loser will therefore pay 150% of the total cost of the lawsuit. In other words, the winner will recover $10,000 of his/her legal costs while the loser will have to pay $30,000. Alice, therefore, thinks she has a 60% chance of only paying $10,000 and getting the diamond and that she has a 40% chance of paying $30,000 and not getting anything. If she wins, after costs, she will have net value of $90,000. But the question is what will Alice pay to achieve certainty and avoid the 40% chance of losing (i.e., paying $30,000 to get nothing?). What if Alice cannot afford to pay $30,000? Now she has a good reason to resolve the matter. The same goes for Bob. No matter who wins, if they don't settle, the net value of the lawsuit looks like this: [Lawyers +40]—[Winner +90]—[Loser -30]. No matter who wins, the lawyers will each charge their client $20,000. The "transaction" cost will be $40,000 paid $10,000 by the winner and $30,000 by the loser.

No two people or companies have the same tolerance for risk, stress, delay, and uncertainty. It is entirely possible that Alice or Bob places a completely different value on possessing the diamond. Say Alice wants the diamond badly because it was her mother's. Bob, her brother, in desperate need of cash, only wants the diamond for its market value of $100,000. If Alice loses, it will cost her $30,000 in legal fees. Because she may want the diamond at all costs, she might well want to buy certainty at a higher price than Bob would offer.

At the point where the mediation occurs, assume Bob and Alice spent approximately $1,000 on legal fees. Even if Alice had a 90% chance of winning, she would be ahead if she paid Bob anything less than $9,000 to end the matter. But because she knows she will have to spend at least $130,000 to possess the diamond if she loses, Alice can tantalize Bob with a very generous offer to settle which, if it is anywhere near $90,000, will seem like total victory to Bob.

Where, as in this case, each concedes the other has a 40% chance of winning, there is a great deal of room to negotiate.

⸭

At some point a broad basis of agreement will begin to suggest itself to the mediator. Identifying the basis and carefully managing it without creating insurmountable barriers is a critical point in the mediation.

Testing the limits of each party's flexibility and perception of reality is the final stage. When the parties have done as much as they can to resolve the matter, an agreement will either be reached or there will be a need for further reflection or input. One of the parties may have reached the point where it is not prepared to move further, having reached their walk-away position. Unless something can be done to alter this state of affairs, the impasse is real and the mediation is over.

If there are serious problems and impasse is reached, it will usually be because one or more of the "Barriers to Success" described in Chapter 5 has been encountered. The work necessary to overcome the barrier will begin and the success of the mediation will depend on the parties' ability to work through them.

VALUABLE NON-MONETARY ELEMENTS OF RESOLUTION

The example of Bob and Alice illustrates how negotiation works when some elements of resolution have real value to your opponent and may cost you little or nothing. To put it another way, your opponent's gain may not be at your expense.

Vindication, saving face, acknowledgement, apology, money now, payment in kind or in services, stress avoidance, legal-fee avoidance, certainty or risk aversion, and business concessions such as volume discounts, rebates, and extended warranties will all be valued differently by individual parties to a negotiation. Avoiding negative publicity or news media attention; avoiding the creation of a bad legal precedent which may be costly and embarrassing; retaining customers and other relationships; and enjoying good press are all further examples of some non-monetary, but very real and valuable, elements consistently overlooked or undervalued in negotiations which can be used to create value on both sides of the table.

If you are alert to the possibilities, only your creativity and the facts of the case limit the value-creating potential that is possible during the course of negotiations. Do not make the mistake that many do in negotiations. Do not look at the dispute entirely from your own perspective or apply only your value system to settlement options.

The key to creating value in a negotiation is to walk in the other side's shoes and imagine you are on the other side of the table. By doing this, you will unearth and be able to mine resources that permit a widening and enriching of the modes of resolution and enable agreement to be reached where none was previously thought possible. That is what negotiation is really all about and that should be your quest. You should continuously ask yourself, "What is really important to the other side, and what do they value?" while at the same time attending to your own needs. In our example, brother Bob really needed cash in a hurry, not a diamond. He would have had to find a buyer (possibly his disgruntled sister), negotiate a price and conclude the sale transaction if he were successful in the lawsuit. Avoiding this had value for Bob. Likewise, Alice didn't want money, she wanted a keepsake of their mother. Having to negotiate with Bob to buy the diamond after losing a court battle would not be a happy prospect for her. Avoiding that has value for Alice.

The following are a number of types of non-monetary factors which often have a disproportionate value to one side in negotiations.

Vindication/Saving Face

When it is clear from listening to the other party that some form of vindication or acknowledgement of their position is important, even recognizing shared or full responsibility may be helpful. Nothing is lost in the confidential atmosphere of mediation by providing acknowledgement or crafting a document which vindicates somebody's position, provided it doesn't impinge upon your interests. I am continuously amazed at the ability of parties to craft press releases which satisfy both sides. In one libel case I asked both sides to draft what they viewed as an appropriate apology and retraction. The apology drafted by the defendant was far more elaborate and complete than the one drafted by the complainant. This graphically illustrated the point for me that often what the other side is prepared to do will far exceed your own expectations.

Saving face may be more important to one side than another. This has a lot to do with emotional components. In many cases, creative ways may be found to give face and save face.

Apology

Apology is perhaps one of the least understood but most powerful negotiation tools. Very little has been written about the value of apology in negotiation. When strong emotions are present, an apology can be tremendously useful. While apologies are free, they must be offered sincerely. Coupled with other aspects of the resolution (for example, money), it is surprising how highly valued an apology may be to someone who feels wronged, if it is given by the appropriate person at the appropriate time.

Money Now vs. Money Later

Like brother Bob, how many of us are happy to wait two or three years or more to resolve a financial claim in the courts? We can all put the money to better use now and would value having it sooner rather than later. The value of money now is not that well understood in negotiation. Individuals, particularly those with little money, may place a high value on early payment. It may be that lawyers don't pay attention to it because they aren't the main beneficiary of early settlement.

I am reminded of the insurance adjuster who always comes to mediations with a chequebook and has authority to write the cheque on the spot. This is a powerful negotiating tool in some cases. The time to negotiate flexible payment terms is not after a court judgement has been obtained. The winner may not be in the mood to be as flexible as you might like.

The corollary of money now is money later. People do not always realize that they may negotiate for payment terms that are favourable to them. Often, psychologically, the amount of money paid is more important to the claimant than the terms of payment. I recall a mediation where the return of the entire deposit in a failed real estate transaction was so important to the plaintiff on moral grounds that he agreed to accept payment over five years with *no* interest. In addition to payment terms, substantial savings may be achieved by paying in kind or by undertaking to provide services.

Stress Avoidance

Ignoring or undervaluing the amount of stress produced by litigation is a major tactical error. People do not like to be involved in a war. Lawyers, insurance adjusters, and others whose livelihood is related to litigation, fail to fully appreciate and properly evaluate the amount of stress felt by their opponents and clients and the corresponding value they place on stress avoidance. I am continually being told (in confidence) by litigants how much the proceeding was affecting their health and ability to enjoy their lives.

Risk Aversion or Certainty

Corporate executives, business people, and just about everyone who isn't a riverboat gambler, will acknowledge that they dislike risk. It is neither stupid nor unbusinesslike to pay a premium to avoid risk. Most business persons see disputes and other business risks in shades of grey. They are quite comfortable making decisions based on realistic probabilities and factoring them into their expectations in defining an appropriate outcome. Because litigation is an all-or-nothing proposition, lawyers focus on their chances of winning the case. However, in negotiations, they do their clients a disservice by not providing conservative and appropriate forecasts of the probability of losing.

Business Concessions

These days businesses that find themselves in a dispute are rarely competitors or mortal enemies. Most often they are customers or suppliers. The costs of generating new customers, as opposed to keeping existing ones intact, are all too well known. If the relationship isn't irrevocably broken, there are untold possibilities for renewing the business relationship. I have witnessed mediations settled on an offer of guaranteed future business at reasonable margins in order to make up losses. Other concessions which may be highly prized on one side of the table and cost very little on the other include volume discounts, rebates, and extended warranties.

Avoiding Bad Publicity

In the heat of battle, the dispute may deteriorate to the point where public mud-slinging occurs between the parties. Because litigation is very public, the media have become very skilled at combing through court documents for stories. A lot of money is then spent on hiring public relations consultants to minimize the damage. Even if one party usually has more to lose from bad publicity than the other, both will suffer.

Public companies have to note all lawsuits in their annual reports. Private companies must note ongoing lawsuits in their audited financial statements. There is no doubt that these disclosures have a negative effect on how the company is viewed by analysts, prospective investors, and lenders. Conversely, removal of these notations must have a corresponding positive value.

Cost Avoidance

Lawyers, including in-house counsel and people involved in the day-to-day conduct of litigation within companies, often fail to fully comprehend the widespread aversion there is to paying legal fees. While the cost of highly trained and experienced counsel may be worth the expenditure, the costs inherent in proceeding with conventional litigation have become staggering. Nowadays, litigants will (and should) pay a premium to their lawyers for early resolution, to avoid such fees.

Recognition should also be given to the fact that winners of lawsuits recover only a percentage of their judgements from disgruntled and uncooperative losers. The high cost of collecting on judgements must also be recognized.

Good Publicity

Some companies and organizations have settled with generous and perhaps unwarranted payments or other terms. Such cases have been written up favourably in the press, including industrial or trade journals which celebrate the company's strong commitment to customer satisfaction. Cases have been settled on the basis that the manufacturer agrees to recall defective goods and to provide a generous extension to the warranty on the product. This has been capitalized upon by the company as proof of their corporate responsibility. Sometimes it *is* possible to make lemonade out of lemons.

Avoiding a Bad Precedent

Once a court has decided a particular case, it may have continuing adverse consequences to a party because of the precedent it sets. In disputes involving interpretations of insurance policies or terminations of employment, for example, subsequent claimants demand the same package previously awarded by the courts. These results may be avoided through mediation and resolution agreements which contain confidentiality clauses.

Mediation is not about simply getting or keeping as much as possible. Everyone wants the best deal. Legitimate business interests do try to maximize profits and people do seek the most favourable results. But disputes are far more complex. No one in a negotiation is motivated by the same things; each party is distinct, possessing unique motives, concerns, values, interests, emotions, and responses. Skilful negotiators able to discern these differences will be in a position to create added value and options for mutual gain, which will result in higher levels of satisfaction than could possibly be achieved in a court process. This is both the challenge and promise of mediation.

STAGE FIVE—RESOLUTION

Incorporating the most attractive options into an agreement is the last stage. At this point the available options are rigorously tested against agreed criteria to ensure that the agreement will satisfy the essential needs of the parties and that the agreement is efficient, fair, durable, and enforceable. These concepts as well as the subject of resolution, generally have entire chapters devoted to them because of their importance (Chapter 6).

During this stage, the mediator will be alert to significant discomfort or unease of a party relating to aspects of the agreement as well as to legitimate concerns relating to the agreement criteria, assisting the parties to creatively overcome last-minute glitches and qualms.

IF AGREEMENT ISN'T POSSIBLE

Sometimes despite the best efforts of everyone, the mediation becomes bogged down or stymied. Consider the likely cause. It may be simply that the session has gone on too long, and everyone is exhausted, hungry, or out of patience. If substantial progress has been made, another session would appear to be warranted.

If the mediation has stalled, it is a good idea to review the issues and the progress made on each. It might be useful for each party to review their walk-away position to ensure nothing has been overlooked and that they are grounded in reality.

What are the unresolved issues and why exactly are they still outstanding? It may be very useful for each party to explain their understanding of the available options on the table. Often there is a misunderstanding, which if clarified, will permit movement. This also allows for refinement or even subtle (or not so subtle) shifting to accommodate the other party when failure looms close on the horizon.

In reviewing the options on the table further options may arise. The mediator may at this point be helpful by floating a number of other possibilities. When the problems are identified consider ways to overcome the barrier.

Case Study

A landlord and tenant of a unit in an industrial mall were fighting over the terms of their agreement. They had initially signed an "offer to lease" which contemplated the negotiation and signing of a lease covering all the details of their relationship. Unfortunately, the landlord had allowed the tenant into possession before this agreement was finalized. The negotiation became protracted over a two-year period. Their relationship deteriorated to the point that the landlord locked the tenant out. The tenant immediately applied to the court for an order restoring the status quo. The court ordered the landlord to permit the tenant to resume his business on terms, including that they try to mediate their differences before returning to court for a final determination.

During the mediation it became clear that each party had a long list of grievances. Because there was no lease, each thought the other was responsible for such things as maintenance and repair of the premises. Use of the common areas and parking lot and who was responsible for the payment of utilities were also issues.

The landlord insisted that the lease was net or care free and the tenant was responsible for all costs attributed to the premises because the "offer to lease" said a net lease would be entered into by the parties. The tenant countered with the argument that they had in fact negotiated a "gross lease" and by their conduct over the past two years, the landlord having accepted rent on that basis was bound by the terms of the unsigned gross lease.

The landlord continued to insist throughout the mediation that the tenant must sign a lease as a minimum term of settling the lawsuit. It became clear that for various reasons, particularly the tenant's perception that no lease provided negotiating leverage with a landlord perceived to be unreasonable, the tenant was not prepared to sign a lease and would take their chances in court.

In the dying minutes of the mediation when things looked pretty bleak, the mediator reviewed the list of key irritants on both sides. Creative and workable solutions had been found for each one. The mediator pointed out that the parties had lived together for two years and had these solutions been in place there would not have been any conflict on those issues. As to future issues, the parties readily agreed to a clause requiring them to negotiate and, if the negotiation failed, to mediate, and if still at loggerheads to arbitrate.

The solutions to the existing problems and ADR clause were incorporated into a written agreement which when completed looked an awful lot like a lease, however, it was called Minutes of Settlement. While both parties were adamant about signing or not signing a lease, they were able to find a way to achieve their goals and bring and end to the hostilities.

In conclusion, where impasse appears unbreakable, both parties should review what leaving the dispute unresolved means for them. It may be that they will agree to a further session after a period of cooling down and reflection. Further work may be necessary. They may need to develop further information through discoveries or further investigations before another session would be productive. On the other hand, the parties may be so intransigent and far apart that the only realistic way of breaking the impasse is to consider arbitration or litigation.

☑ Mediation Process Checklist

❑ Stage One   **Convening Stage**

Have all necessary parties been identified and have they agreed to participate? Do they have the required authority?

Has all the information necessary for the negotiation been assembled, developed, and exchanged?

Has a written summary or mediation brief of each party's position been prepared containing their proposals?

Is the date, time, and place of the first meeting settled? Will more than one session be necessary? If so, are they to take place consecutively or on different dates?

Are the ground rules understood and agreed on? Has the Agreement to Mediate been signed by everyone? Is there any need to meet beforehand to settle any of the rules of proceeding?

Are the accommodations adequate for the joint sessions and caucuses? Are there dry boards, flip charts, video, conferencing, if needed, telephone, fax, food, and beverages close at hand?

❑ Stage Two   **Introductions and Ground Rules**

Formal introductions of the mediator and parties. A detailed exploration of the process (roles of parties, mediator, ground rules, confidentiality, matters relating to intention and authority, rules about caucus meetings, questions or comments) led by the mediator.

❑ Stage Three   **Information Exchange and Issue Identification**

Opening statements, clarification and simplification, questions and answers. Is all the information at hand or is more needed?

Is an adjournment appropriate while new information is gathered? Is an expert necessary?

Should there be a caucus? Should there be another joint session? All issues should be defined.

❏ **Stage Four   Problem Solving**

Strike an agenda, brainstorm, generate options. Test options against specific criteria. Adjust as many as necessary.

❏ **Stage Five   Resolution**

Incorporate acceptable options after testing against agreed criteria for a good agreement. (See Chapter 6.)

Is ratification or independent legal advice necessary?

❏ **If Agreement Isn't Possible:**

Review progress and summarize. Review walk-away position of each party.

Review and identify issues not resolved and why. Return to Stage Three with these issues. Examine each party's perceptions of the options relating to the unresolved issue. Do they see the opinion as efficient, fair, durable, and enforceable? Generate more options.

Consider barriers checklist and identify problem.

Consider ending the mediation with the parties and explore what that means to them. Are there any other process options available?

Consider further discussions and whether another session would be productive, and if so, on what terms.

4

THE ROLE OF MEDIATORS AND LAWYERS

$\mathbf{M}$ediators come from all walks of life. Everyone mediates every day between colleagues, family, and friends. In one sense mediation is an age-old profession, practised by village elders, shamans, religious and community leaders. Children mediate among themselves. There are now formal programmes in some schools teaching our children how to resolve conflict by using "peer mediation." Some mediators have gained a reputation for excellence in their communities and are called upon as needed. Mediators specializing in business and commercial disputes tend to be lawyers, accountants, engineers, and management consultants.

Certain professions have gravitated towards family mediation—notably health care providers, such as psychologists and psychiatrists—presumably because of the high emotional content and lasting effects of these disputes. Social workers and social service providers also make a large contribution to the profession.

Because of its diversity, the profession is completely unregulated and divided on the issues of accreditation and regulation for a variety of reasons. Some mediators are part-time, others practise full-time. Some specialize in community, cultural conflict, and school disputes, while others provide family mediation as an adjunct to their medical or legal practice. There are mediators who are principally trainers of would-be mediators, while still others restrict their practices to commercial and business disputes.

Some observers dismiss the debate over standards and accreditation as merely turf wars between various professionals. However, I believe the heart of the issue resides in the very nature of mediation and ADR. Historically and currently, the choice of mediator has always been left to the parties for the very good reason that they know better than anyone else who is likely to assist them resolve *their* dispute. The matter of free choice of mediator is central to the process. But what about quality control and consumer protection from "instant mediators?"

Everyone agrees that it is critical that mediators be qualified. But no one agrees what standards to apply or what sort of training and experience should form a baseline minimum requirement for accreditation. Even if they did, since mediators come from all professions and walks of life, who will regulate this new profession? The government, in this day and age of smaller government, would have to step in to create an umbrella mediator regulation regime or each profession interested in the field would have to create separately or jointly, regulations for their membership. This would still leave a large number of highly competent veteran mediators, who are not members of a recognized profession, to their own devices and the mediation community would be the poorer for it. They might in turn band together and create their own standards and system of accreditation, however, this is unlikely in the near future.

MANDATORY COURT-CONNECTED MEDIATION

If the courts and legal administrators of the provinces mandate mediation in the early stages of a lawsuit, their ability to control the mediators is absolute because at this point, mediation has become a "justice product." As such, they have a public duty to ensure high-level and consistent process quality and uniformity in mediation style, competence, and experience.

In Ontario the court-connected programme proposes setting up a roster in each of the province's regions. Generally, to be accepted for the roster, a candidate will have to provide acceptable evidence of:

- mediation training;
- mediation experience;
- familiarity with the civil litigation system;
- other factors including teaching or training; and
- contributions to the literature or the profession.

It appears the universe of mediation is unfolding as it should. It is an emerging profession having broad applications across the range of human experience. Since the ability of the parties to choose their own mediator must be inviolate and no one group can lay claim to the sum of mediator wisdom, a state of uncertainty is probably best in order to allow the process of evolution to continue unfettered.

While this may all be well and good in principle, it certainly is of little assistance in the short term to someone considering mediation now. The balance of this chapter is devoted to the practical business of assisting you to select a mediator and lawyer by discussing in detail their respective roles in the mediation process.

ROLE OF THE MEDIATOR

In order to better understand which mediator to choose, you should have a good idea of the mediator's role during the process. The mediator:

- controls and shapes the process;
- ensures a safe environment;
- is neutral, unbiased, and unconnected in any way with the parties, their lawyers, or the dispute;
- assists the parties as a coach to negotiate in a realistic and principled manner;
- understands the emotional undercurrents, but isn't swept away by them;
- persists when an impasse is reached with helpful suggestions, questions, and other techniques to overcome the deadlock; and
- keeps the parties and counsel focused and moving towards agreement.

QUALITIES OF A GOOD MEDIATOR

There are two essential qualities of a good mediator. One I call EQ, or empathy quotient, is the ability to appreciate a party's point of view without agreeing with it. Other important characteristics in this regard will include the ability to listen, emotional stability, maturity, and sensitivity. Another essential quality is IQ, or intelligence quotient, the ability to quickly comprehend subtleties relating both to the subject matter of the dispute and what is of real significance to the parties. Additional helpful qualities include patience, persistence, high integrity, and the ability to build rapport quickly.

The mediator must not have any connection with the parties. Any conflict, even a perceived one, must be communicated honestly at the outset. Parties in mediation and counsel are hypersensitive to bias. Any party who picks up on a lack of neutrality will head for the hills and the mediation will fail.

Other things to consider in a mediator include history, experience, and training.

History

Is the mediator a full-time professional or just part-time? If he is a lawyer, what sort of work does he do? Does he always act for the plaintiff or insurance defence or for labour or management in labour disputes? How will that likely affect his ability to be impartial? If the mediator is a full-time practitioner, what was his previous occupation and background? If the mediator is a former insurance adjuster, will his knowledge of the insurance industry be of more benefit than the fact that his perspective may be biased in favour of insurance companies? If the mediator is a litigator or retired judge, will he be able to leave his tendency to form opinions at home and assume the non-judgemental role required of a mediator?

Experience and Training

Experience and training are very important—the more the better. If the training is limited, the level of experience is that much more important. Is the mediator certified? If so, what does that mean—a forty-hour course or intensive formal training by a well-regarded organization and supervision over a number of years? A number of universities in Canada are providing mediator training through their extension departments. These include the University of Prince Edward Island, University of Windsor, York University, Ottawa University, Carleton University, and the University of Toronto. Check with your local university or community college.

Highly respected institutions in Canada that provide quality training in conflict resolution and process design include the Justice Institute in British Columbia and the Canadian International Institute of Applied Negotiation in Ottawa. Look for a certificate from a respected institution following an intensive course of study and practical experience. Find out what the certificate really means. A credible certificate will involve having taken several courses over several months, if not years. As we have seen, mediation is an unregulated profession. Anyone can hang out a shingle and call themselves a mediator. Is she a member of a recognized professional group or association? Some respected professional groups include: the Arbitration and Mediation Institute of Canada, Family Mediation Canada, the Network for Conflict Resolution and the Society of Professionals in Dispute Resolution.

Who are the mediator's references? Check them. Do they include satisfied customers? How many mediations has she *conducted*, not just attended? What types of mediations were they? One enthusiastic mediator claimed to have mediated "hundreds" of cases. It turned out that the vast majority of these were "mediated" over the telephone and related to customer complaints. How many cases similar to yours has the mediator handled? How does the mediator generally work? Does she have the ability and training to design a process that suits your particular dispute? Interview the mediator at length. At the end of this chapter, I have provided an interview guide checklist.

MUST THE MEDIATOR HAVE KNOWLEDGE OF THE ISSUES?

The mediator needs to develop quickly an understanding of the legal and technical issues in the dispute. However, because he is not deciding anything and should not intrude with an opinion, detailed technical knowledge may, in fact, be a problem if it gets in the way of the parties' own ability to design a solution that suits them. A mediator selected solely for technical expertise rather than mediation skill will naturally assume that it is his opinion on the issues which is of paramount importance to the parties. While this is true in arbitration, it is not the case in mediation where the emphasis should be on assisting the parties to come to their own agreement. For example, a lawyer, expert in employment law with no mediation credentials, hired by the parties to mediate a wrongful dismissal case, may focus exclusively on whether the employer had "just cause" to fire the employee. If he agrees with the employer's arguments, the fact that the parties simply want to resolve their problem might be overlooked, and the employer, having received further support from the mediator, might be less inclined to resolve the matter in a way that suits both parties.

If the matter is highly technical, some expertise may be of assistance, provided the mediator has, above all, strong mediating skills and experience. If, for example, the matter involves complex legal and technical points in a dispute about cost overruns and construction methods, the mediator should be able to understand the issues in order to properly guide the process, and be of assistance in helping the parties avoid legal pitfalls. It should be stressed, however, that the parties' lawyers must always be the prime resource in the avoidance of pitfalls in mediation. Mediators should *never* offer legal advice.

It should be remembered in this connection that:

- The parties have their own technical experts and the ability to acquire technical advice. The parties are negotiating an agreement to address their interests, not someone else's concept of them.

- Offering an opinion immediately puts the mediator's neutrality in question.

- The mediation process puts pressure on both sides to be reasonable and realistic. When there is a wide gulf between them, it is usually because key information is being misapprehended or isn't available. The mediator is not the appropriate source of this information. Experts are.

DOES THE MEDIATOR HAVE TO HAVE INSURANCE?

Does the mediator carry liability insurance? Most lawyers who mediate will be insured under their professional liability insurance programmes. This is a matter about which you should enquire. What sort of insurance is it? Does it afford protection for the mediator's negligent acts or omissions? While there is little experience in mediator negligence to date, one can envision cases of dishonesty or negligence where a mediator has an undeclared conflict of interest or conspires with one of the parties to the mediation, causing losses to the other. These days, all eventualities should be protected against. Failure to carry this kind of insurance will speak volumes about the mediator's business acumen, if nothing else. You should not have to bear the risk of mediator incompetence or dishonesty.

STYLE OF THE MEDIATOR

Mediators differ greatly in style and this can be critical in the mediation. Choosing a mediator whose style is compatible with both parties' objectives is important. Degrees of directiveness will vary. The trend is towards mediators who favour an interest-based negotiation. Interest-based negotiation adopts a problem-solving approach based on objective standards. The parties are encouraged to express their respective needs, concerns, and aspirations, and work together towards a result that is mutually satisfactory based on the merits of their respective cases.

Directive Mediation

You must decide how hands-on you want the mediator to be. Some people favour a very directive approach where the mediator guides the parties to a resolution. This approach is defined earlier as "Rights-Based Mediation." This style of mediation puts a premium on the mediator's knowledge and experience and ability to comprehend fully all nuances and intricacies of the dispute, including the way the parties feel about it in a very short period of time without the benefit of hearing witnesses or examining the evidence. A tall order.

Is the mediator an ex-judge or trial lawyer? This may be helpful if you wish the mediator to play a strongly directive role and provide you with an opinion on who will win the case, but it may not be helpful if you wish the mediator to be less interventionist and allow you and your counterpart to control the outcome.

One risk of employing an excessively directive mediator is poor user satisfaction. This is because in this process the parties are shunted to the side in favour of guidance from the mediator. Mediation is voluntary and it should not feel coercive. On the other hand, where it is so important to one or both parties to have someone of obvious stature as a precondition to agreeing to mediate—for example, a high profile ex-judge or lawyer—these considerations are less important than is agreement to proceed with the process.

Interest-Based Mediation

In contrast to the directive style is an interest-based approach, where, as we have seen, the mediator assists the parties to state their needs and encourages them to generate creative options to satisfy both sides. The mediator intervenes only when necessary: to help overcome barriers or assist in the creative process. The style of the mediator may be hands-on and far from "touch feely" in dealing with unrealistic positions or expectations, but the mediator's opinion is not, and should not be substituted for that of the parties.

Even among interest-based mediators, the spectrum of style varies greatly from mediator to mediator. These can range from mildly interventionist to very hands-on, depending on the parties, the stage of the mediation and the type of dispute. The former style has been described as "hasher" and the latter, "trasher." The hasher acts as a facilitator ensuring the parties completely understand one another. The so-called trasher, on the other hand, is much more active in the process particularly in the latter stages, challenging, questioning, and exhorting the parties to review their positions in light of reasonable objective parameters. Rather than hasher and trasher, I prefer the less graphic but more descriptive terms "facilitative" and "evaluative."

Some mediators favour a style where they move from group to group, carefully controlling the exchanges through a form of shuttle diplomacy. Others prefer that the parties remain together for the duration of the mediation, communicating directly with one another. An experienced mediator will design a process to suit the dynamics of the specific dispute. A good mediator should be able to shift chameleon-like from one style to another. His style should be determined not by personality, but rather by the requirements of the mediation as it unfolds.

The mediator earns the right during the mediation to be more involved by gaining the trust and respect of the parties. It is the parties who should invite heightened involvement by the mediator, not the other way around.

MEDIATOR ETHICS

The integrity of the mediator is the essential heart of the mediation process. Skill levels may vary, but parties to a mediation have a right to a consistently high level of integrity in their mediator.

Coercion

The mediator must not impose a result or her views on how the dispute should be resolved. Whether or not to resolve, and on what basis, is for the parties involved to decide, not the mediator. Too much emphasis on "settlement rates" suggests the mediator may not be comfortable with the possibility that the parties may choose not to settle.

Mediators Must Not Provide Legal Advice or an Opinion

The mediator should not provide legal advice. However, the mediator may provide negotiation coaching. That is very different. Also, asking a mediator for an opinion on who will probably win or lose in court is improper. Providing a response is inappropriate unless both parties request it and the mediator feels comfortable giving it.

Impartiality

Is the mediator capable of remaining even-handed and impartial? For example, is a former excavation contractor capable of being impartial in a mediation between a disputing general contractor and an excavating contractor? Is a school trustee capable of mediating between a school board and a teacher? It is crucial to choose a mediator who is impartial.

Conflict of Interest

The mediator should have no past or current association with any of the parties. Members of same golf or social club, a distant relative by marriage, or children who play hockey together are all examples of potential conflicts.

Mediator Must Respect Confidences

A mediator who is conducting a legal practice may be deemed in law to share information received in the course of that practice with his partners. This may create problems with respect to confidentiality. If sensitive or confidential information is being shared with the mediator, the mediator may have to agree that his firm will not accept any future litigation assignments involving parties to the mediation. Anything learned by the mediator during the mediation process must never be revealed by the mediator outside the process without the parties' permission.

Integrity of the Process

A mediator must, to the best of her ability, ensure the highest possible process quality. If the mediator suspects a party is not negotiating in good faith, the matter should be dealt with, and if not rectified, the mediation should be terminated. An example would be using the mediation process as a means of gathering information and learning more about the opponent's case, with no real intention to resolve the matter, rather simply to get the upper hand in a lawsuit.

Rarely will information revealed during a mediation not emerge during the discovery process. If, however, highly sensitive information is used in the mediation that would not have to be revealed during the normal litigation discovery process, and that information is used subsequently during the trial to the detriment of the party who revealed it in good faith, in my view a clear breach of the confidentiality agreement has occurred. This would give rise to a claim for damages. Also, a plea to the judge hearing the case might result in the evidence being excluded. Clearly parties to mediation must assess the benefits of sharing sensitive information against the prospects of it being used improperly. During mediations as with negotiation, the parties continuously assess each other and their comfort level with the other's motives and trustworthiness. In certain cases it is appropriate to get a pre-agreement in writing that the shared information will not be used if the mediation fails.

HOW TO FIND THE RIGHT MEDIATOR

Now that you know what you are looking for in a mediator, the next question is how to locate one that fits your requirements.

Buyer Beware

Because the provision of mediation services and mediators are completely unregulated, "Buyer Beware" should apply. Locating the right mediator requires the same diligence as you might expend on finding the right architect, doctor, or lawyer. Generally, you will rely on the people you trust—a colleague, your lawyer, a family member, or trusted friend—for a referral. It is precisely because the area is unregulated and standards for accreditation vary so widely that the earlier part of this chapter focused largely on assisting you to do your own "due diligence."

Mediation has caught the imagination of some individuals who have simply added the title to their business card and résumé in the hope of increasing their business. The fact that they may lack training, related experience, and integrity is a major concern. Having said that, there are plenty of highly reputable, well-trained and experienced mediators to choose from.

Mediation Service Providers

These companies are springing up almost daily across the country. They maintain rosters of mediators. You should ask whether or not the principals of the company are mediators or whether the company simply acts as a broker or agent who convenes the mediation and attends to administrative details for a fee.

Mediator Associations

In Canada there are three well-recognized mediator associations which maintain membership lists. They provide their membership with continuing education and networking opportunities. The Arbitration and Mediation

Institute of Canada maintains a membership list of both arbitrators and mediators who meet their criteria based on experience and training. Family Mediation Canada, based in Guelph, Ontario, is the established family mediation association. The Network for Conflict Resolution is a mediator trade association based in Conrad Grebel College at the University of Waterloo.

Court Rosters

As mentioned earlier, several provinces are considering a mandatory requirement that mediation be used before lawsuits are permitted to proceed through the traditional system of discoveries, pretrials, and trials. Ontario began implementing its programme in 1997. It is anticipated that others will follow suit.

Because mediation is compulsory as part of the justice system in Ontario, there will be a requirement that mediators pass the scrutiny of the Ministry of the Attorney-General based on the requirements listed on pages 89-90. This will ensure minimum standards of training, experience, suitability, and accountability. However, the choice of mediator will still be yours. While some comfort should be derived from the knowledge that the mediator's name appears on the roster, the onus is on you to select one who is suitable for your purposes.

Referral Service

Most of the lawyers' governing bodies in Canada maintain referral services. In addition, some provincial arms of the Canadian Bar Association publish a list of lawyers who have an interest in the area of Alternative Dispute Resolution. These lawyers may be full- or part-time mediators or merely have an interest in ADR. You will need to inquire further to ensure you are dealing with a qualified mediator.

There is no substitute for doing your homework in selecting a mediator. So much of mediation depends on neutrality, fairness, trust, and skill that considerable attention should be devoted to the choice. Confidence can best be achieved by a careful process of selection that includes an interview and the checking of references and credentials.

Take an active role in selecting the mediator. If you leave the choice to others, indicate your preferences as to style. For example, if you think a more interest-based mediator would suit you, say so.

ROLE OF THE LAWYER

The role of the lawyer in a mediation is entirely different than it is in court. While a court trial is a lawyer's show as directed by the judge, mediation is the parties' show as structured by the mediator in consultation with all parties including the lawyer, if you choose to have her present.

Prior to and during the mediation, your lawyer will be of assistance by providing:

- assistance in selecting the mediator, if you require it;
- active and cooperative involvement in setting up the mediation and working out the important logistics with the other counsel and the mediator;
- advice concerning the law and assisting you in avoiding any legal pitfalls;
- an objective valuation of the position of your opponent and a well considered, conservative opinion of the strengths and weaknesses of both your case and that of your opponent and avoiding bottom lines which remove flexibility;
- participation in the negotiation as a member of your team;
- feedback concerning what has been said and his interpretation of the information;
- emotional support and a cooler head if things get a bit hot;
- continuous attention to what is going on, working with the client during breaks and not just making phone calls; and
- assistance in drafting an agreement that will be effective, enforceable, and reflect your expectations.

The same degree of care should be applied to the choice of a lawyer as in choosing the mediator. A lawyer who is aggressive and negative toward your opponent or not familiar with the process is the wrong one to take to mediation. If, for instance, you know that your lawyer has already antagonized the other side using intemperate language in the pleadings or at discoveries, consider whether that lawyer should be replaced for the purposes of the mediation.

Your lawyer should be willing to work as part of your team in preparing for the mediation. If your lawyer thinks the sole reason for having you along at the mediation is to provide encouragement and instructions, she is not the right choice. Similarly, if the lawyer thinks you should speak when she says so or tries to filter what you feel or want to say to the mediator, you may also want to reconsider your choice.

Your lawyer should have considerable expertise in negotiation and mediation. He should have taken the trouble to receive training and have unquestioned credentials as a negotiator. Has he taken care to completely familiarize himself with the rules governing the mediation if it is court connected and explained the process to you in detail? These questions will be answered by the quality of and priority placed on preparation. Courtesy, tact, and personality don't hurt either.

Remember, you are paying the lawyer's fees. Interview your lawyer as rigorously as you would a prospective mediator. If your lawyer is sceptical about using mediation in your case, check the reasons advanced against those set out in Chapter 2. Do they make sense?

In short, the ideal lawyer is one who sees the client's broad interests as paramount and who does not regard the mediation process as depriving her of a lucrative file. If you sense a problem while interviewing your lawyer, it's time to look around.

LEGAL ETHICS IN MEDIATION

Even if the conduct is not specifically prohibited by the codes of ethics, lawyers should nevertheless reflect on the practical ramifications of difficult behaviour during negotiation. Such behaviour, whether or not it is officially reported, is unofficially broadcast on the lawyer network and can therefore be career limiting.

Equally important to clients is the lawyer's duty to warn clients against accepting a bad proposal which does not meet their minimum needs. Rarely, but too often, a lawyer may urge acceptance of a clearly inadequate proposal for reasons unrelated to the client's best interests, and related more to the lawyer's interest in being paid. Fortunately these lawyers are in the minority. This, however, illustrates the importance in taking care when choosing your lawyer.

The following are a few points on legal ethics in mediation that you should keep in mind:

- The lawyer is an officer of the court even during a mediation and is bound by a professional code of ethics established by the jurisdiction in which he practises. While courageous advocacy is expected, honesty, fairness, and courtesy should temper and inform the lawyer's behaviour during the mediation. The conduct of the lawyer should never be a barrier to agreement.

- The lawyer should provide the client with a closely reasoned and accurate assessment of the risks and costs of litigation without overestimating or underestimating the case, and revise it during the mediation if fairness and reasonableness dictate.

- Since unrealistic expectations are perhaps the single most frequently encountered barrier to successful negotiation, the lawyer must not encourage the client's expectations unduly. Instead the lawyer should assist the client by being realistic and, if necessary, use the mediator as an ally to temper the expectations of an overly optimistic client.

- Lawyers should lead by example by being cooperative and candid with their counterparts. They should encourage their clients to be equally forth-coming and explain to the client beforehand that the confidentiality agree-ment is in place to both encourage openness and protect against taking undue advantage of anything revealed during the process.

- It goes without saying that lawyers should refrain from misleading the mediator, her counterpart, or the opponents.

The Canadian Bar Association Code of Professional Conduct, under the heading Compromise or Settlement, states:

> The lawyer should advise and encourage the client to compromise or settle a dispute whenever possible on a reasonable basis and should discourage the client from commencing or continuing useless legal proceedings.

I am not aware of any guidance from the courts or the Canadian Bar Associ-ation on what constitutes "useless legal proceedings," although I suspect a number of defendants would be pleased to elaborate. Ultimately it is the courts and lawyers' governing bodies that define what is useless by penaliz-ing those lawyers who bring frivolous lawsuits by awarding significant costs against them personally and, in extreme cases, disbarring them.

In Ontario, a subcommittee of the lawyers' governing body, the Law Society of Upper Canada, recommended in February 1993 that the rules of professional conduct be amended to place a positive obligation on lawyers *to inform their clients of alternatives to litigation and to respond to proposals for the use of alternative methods of dispute resolution.*

On May 24, 1996, a much watered-down version was adopted as an amendment to Rule 10 of the Rules of Professional Conduct:

> The lawyer should consider the appropriateness of ADR to the resolution of issues in every case and, if appropriate the lawyer should inform the client of ADR options and, if so instructed, take steps to pursue those options.

Given that there appears to be some lingering ambivalence towards mediation in the legal profession, it may be up to you to evaluate the appro-priateness of your case and provide your lawyer with the necessary instruc-tions. If she balks at mediation, perhaps a second opinion is in order.

☑ Interview Guide Checklist

STYLE OF MEDIATOR

❑ Interest-based
1. Facilitative
2. Evaluative

Does the mediator favour one form
of mediation? If so, which one?

❑ Directive

INTERVIEW WITH MEDIATOR

❑ Full-time/Part-time Mediator

❑ Interpersonal Skills, IQ, EQ   Listening skills. My impressions.

❑ Experience   How many mediations conducted?
What types of mediation? Any like mine?

❑ Knowledge and Background   Do they compliment my needs?

❑ Communication Skills   Am I convinced? Verbal and non-verbal skills.

❑ Training and Education   Is he involved in training and taking
Professional Certificates   additional courses? Which institutions?
and Organization   Type and length of courses? Was there a
peer review by qualified mediators?

❑ Written Materials   Are they professional looking? Are they clear,
well-organized, and well-written?

❑ Fees   Explore these items in detail. Usually all parties share
the costs equally. Is there an hourly rate, daily
minimum and maximum, any cancellation fee? What
about out-of-pocket expenses, preparation time?

❑ Timing   When will the mediation occur? Will there be any
problem scheduling a second session if needed?
Remember, the beauty of mediation is its timeliness.
If the mediator is backed up for six months, should
you be considering alternatives?

❑ Location   Where will the mediation take place? Is the space
neutral and suitable with private rooms and access
to amenities?

❑ Insurance   Does it cover mediator liability for negligence?

❑ Other Concerns   Are there any potential conflicts? What does the
                            mediator do when not mediating? Does she know
                            the other party, their lawyer? On what basis?
                            Who are the mediator's clients? Is she frequently
                            nominated by insurance companies, contractors,
                            injured persons? Does this matter to me?

SELECTION OF MEDIATOR

❑ References

    (1) _____   Who are the mediator's references? Do they include
                            satisfied parties as well as lawyers. Is there experience
    (2) _____   with similar disputes? Check the references. It is
                            appropriate to ask whether there is any business or
    (3) _____   other relationship between the mediator and the
                            reference. How many occasions has the mediator
                            been used by this law firm or party? Past clients will
                            give the most meaningful assessments. Be sceptical of
                            extravagant claims. You may also wish to check
                            claims relating to training and experience. Unfortun-
                            ately, there are charlatans in this field as in others.

5 BARRIERS TO SUCCESS

I have identified fourteen of the most common barriers to success in mediation. This list is not intended to be exhaustive. It is based on my experience which is primarily with disputes already embroiled in litigation.

Barriers to success are different than impasses. Impasses may result when the parties have exhausted their ability or willingness to meet each other's needs. Barriers are hurdles which must be surmounted during the course of the mediation which, if unaddressed, will usually result in impasse and failure to reach agreement.

Difficult people and difficult behaviour are dealt with separately because while anger may be the cause of the difficulty, there may be a lot of other reasons causing the problem.

ANGER

I have selected anger as the first barrier to successful mediation because of my experiences mediating cases where the parties had commenced litigation prior to agreeing on mediation. How far into the litigation process can mediation be effective? My own view is that generally the further down the litigation road the parties travel, the more difficult it is to turn the boat around. It has momentum. It's in litigation mode.

While emotion plays a role in any dispute, when a conflict escalates to the point where lawyers are the only means of getting someone's attention, fierce emotions are guaranteed. In private session, disputants often confide to the mediator that the real motivation for the litigation is anger, at least partially. They are often loath to talk about any of this directly with their opponent, even though such a discussion would better enable their adversary to understand what is driving the litigation.

TIP While there may be few common denominators from one dispute to the next, anger or other strong emotions are usually present. Emotions should be recognized as playing a central part in any negotiation. Failure to acknowledge them may be costly and result in failure.

Invariably, anger is almost always present in insurance cases. People with insurance expect to be compensated, fully and immediately. Personal injury and disability claims come to mind where the plaintiffs sit silently with heads down. Doctors use the word "insult." These people have suffered a physical insult to their personal well-being and that of their families. This insult is compounded by their perception of a lack of recognition of their dilemma by the insurance company. The physical insult becomes an emotional one as well. Needless to say, it is not surprising that these two factors create anger in the plaintiffs, which has to be addressed if resolution is to be achieved.

I recall a case involving a father who attended a mediation on behalf of his forty-year-old son. The son's injuries started out as a short-term disability involving a problem with eyesight and depression. During the three years leading up to the mediation, these symptoms eventually developed into a full-blown psychosis. The son was confined to a wheelchair and spent the mediation muttering guttural sounds. His condition required the retired father and mother to give up their normal lives in order to care for their totally disabled son whose claim had been treated as fraudulent by the insurance company, based on erroneous surveillance evidence.

Denial or suppression of these feelings by the mediator, the opposing party, or their lawyer will cause problems in the mediation for several reasons:

• Anger is a genuine, often positive, human emotion that results from feeling hurt, humiliated, betrayed, rejected or threatened, either personally or economically.

• Anger results from frustration when we are being asked to compromise our interests and rights, whether legal or human.

- Anger results when we feel cheated or ripped off by individuals, the system, friends, relatives, business partners, life partners, or children.
- In polite society, we are urged to ignore or suppress anger. We constantly deny that we are angry. Whenever I hear, "it's a matter of principle," I have a strong clue that anger is involved.

There is nothing wrong with feeling angry, any more than there is with feeling sleepy. Anger is perfectly acceptable, and in many ways may be a productive emotion. For example, it helps us to protect ourselves when we are at risk. What is unproductive is giving in to anger and giving vent to it by using intemperate language, gestures, and actions. Examples might include storming out of a room, slamming a briefcase shut, hurling something (even an epithet) at another party. Expressions of anger must be made at the appropriate time and place and should not destroy the negotiation.

How to Recognize Anger in Yourself and Others

The need to recognize anger in ourselves is obvious, but it is equally important to recognize it in others. This is a critical skill because when people are at the peak of anger they cannot hear or understand anything you say. Recognizing the signs of anger in the context of a negotiation is important. Flushed face, agitated body movements, turning away, and uncontrolled interruption are but a few examples.

There is a difference between feigned anger and the real thing. There are also differences in intensity. Mild anger such as impatience, annoyance, or irritability, is common enough and may be useful in negotiation. In contrast, there is anger—rage really—that comes from betrayal, resentment, hatred, and disappointment—the kind that simmers under the surface of many disputes. This type of anger is very negative because it drives the dispute and litigation. This is the more powerful sort of anger that prompts immoderate behaviour. "I'd rather pay my lawyer than that son of a bitch."

In negotiation, it is important to keep tabs on yourself and everyone else so that you *understand* where their anger, and yours, is coming from. If you are able to identify yours, you will be able to articulate your needs in a constructive way. Identify the source of theirs, and you will be well on your way to understanding the source of their anger and a resolution of the dispute.

While these strategies are highly successful when employed by negotiators and during mediation, they will also be used by the mediator. Leave confrontation to the mediator. Occasionally it will be necessary to identify extreme and unproductive behaviour that threatens to derail the mediation. In these cases the mediator will calmly identify the behaviour and set parameters about what isn't acceptable and what will occur if it continues.

What to Do about Your Own Anger

Know yourself, your hot buttons, and the matters in dispute that are particularly annoying to you. Sit down before going into a mediation and clearly articulate these points. Consider what you will do if you are triggered. Perhaps take a break; for example, use some pretext to get a glass of water.

When dealing with your own anger, you should focus on what *you* set out to accomplish in the negotiation. Remind yourself of your objectives and their importance. The bottom line in dealing with anger is taking care of yourself first. Don't allow yourself to be derailed from your objectives in the mediation by anger.

In any dispute, there is a lot of letting go that has to happen before settlement is possible. Letting go of emotions that are bound up in the dispute—whether they are feelings of anger, betrayal or resentment—is of paramount importance in achieving closure. Understand this and be prepared to do your share.

What to Do when Confronted by an Angry Opponent

In the face of anger, most people retreat or attack. We react negatively to anger because we are afraid. This is both instinctual and learned behaviour. People experiencing full-blown anger are not in control because powerful chemicals are being released in their brain. Since it is not possible to reason, or sometimes even to hear, when this is going on, it is not possible to process information. Obviously that is not a good situation for conducting interest-based negotiations.

When this happens, an excellent strategy is to simply take a break. This allows the individual to cool off and return to reason. Some call it "going to the balcony." Others call it a "time-out." I call it taking care of yourself. If you encounter anger during the mediation from an opponent or lawyer, tips for dealing with it include:

TIP   Validate or agree with your opponent by taking a proper share of responsibility. Say something like, "You have a right to be annoyed. Acting peremptorily to change suppliers was inconsiderate." Apologize, but only if you are able to do so with sincerity.

Probe to better understand the underlying causes. Show you are interested, but don't try to stifle the anger. Say something like, "I'd like to know more about that."

Empathize, indicate that you understand and walk in the other person's shoes. You don't have to agree with them to do this. Say something like, "I understand how you might feel that way."

Silence is golden. Pay close attention, show respect, and don't do as some people do and meet anger with a wall of words.

Build rapport. Don't look afraid. Be open, interested, and friendly.

Something that has been of great assistance to me in understanding and dealing with strong emotions is an old proverb: "They are not yelling at you, they are yelling for themselves."

Anger and Mediation

A skilful mediator will divine the root of the anger and assist the parties in talking about it in a productive and safe manner, intervening only when angry behaviour threatens to derail the process. Often workable options involving apologies result in eliminating or lessening these feelings. The mediation provides valuable opportunity to give expression to these feelings and provides a necessary catharsis enabling the parties to move on to address other issues.

The Myth of Litigation

Many lawsuits result from the suppression and denial of anger. The lawyer is our surrogate and champion who will trounce our opponent, legally. The judge will administer the *coup de grâce* and vindicate our position with a lengthy discourse in a well-reasoned, scathing denunciation of our adversary, from which we will derive enormous satisfaction. This is the myth of litigation in our culture.

In truth, the law of averages dictates that a lawyer, even if he is highly competent, wins at trial only slightly more than half the time. A few highly gifted and equally expensive lawyers may do slightly better. Judges are busy, overworked, and often overwhelmed. They are unaware, unimpressed by, or do not permit us to express anger. In their decisions judges rarely assign blame or culpability. They speak of legal liability, a rather antiseptic concept. Usually a court judgement is nothing more than a three-line written endorsement on a trial record—hardly the kind of vindication that people who believe the myth expect. And that only occurs two or three years after the litigation was commenced. By then, the anger is tempered by pain. This includes the pain of having to endure motions, cross-examinations, and legal accounts amounting to thousands of dollars. No wonder even the winners are sometimes angry.

BOTTOM LINES

I wish I had a dollar for every time I heard, "What I really hate about mediation is that the minute I say a number, it becomes the base, and my opponent thinks it's just an opening position to be ratcheted up, up, and up. I don't fool around, I just give my number and that's it."

This attitude says to me as a mediator that the speaker hasn't come to negotiate and may not understand the process. While having a walk-away position is necessary in evaluating any proposed agreement, the thinking that produces bottom lines ignores the other parties' needs or concerns. This approach tends to focus only on getting or keeping as much as possible. It is arrogant because it suggests that you know exactly what is important to them or that you don't care, even before hearing from them. This kind of take-it-or-leave-it approach is not constructive and is unlikely to produce agreement. People who employ this form of negotiation like to think of themselves as hard-nosed negotiators. In truth, it is lazy and unbusinesslike. It suggests a lack of preparation and understanding of interest-based negotiation, or for that matter, any form of negotiation.

I have rarely seen a bottom line that was just that. Usually this type of negotiator will table several bottom lines even during a three- or four-hour mediation. As the trial approaches, or new information emerges, new offers are made. This approach also assumes that only money is of real importance to the other party and disregards other important factors, such as a need for vindication, anger, or business considerations.

I'll never forget the story of the negotiators who broke off negotiations when they heard mediation was being proposed. They were worried that if they continued the "this-is-my-bottom-line" dialogue, there would be nothing left to discuss at the mediation. The variation on this theme is, "If I give my best number now, I won't have anything more to offer on the court-house steps."

Heck, It Really Is Only about Money

Often the parties and their lawyers approach the mediation on the basis of "Read my lips, it's only about the money" or in the words of Rod Tidwell in the movie *Jerry Maguire*, their instructions to their lawyer are "SHOW ME THE MONEY!!" They have a number in mind based on their expectations and analysis. The costs they've incurred up to that point will also feature prominently in the analysis and they approach the mediation cautiously, almost guardedly. They see the mediator as a threat to their aspirations. They are worried that they may be taken advantage of. This leads to a reluctance to participate and general feelings of resentment, sometimes expressed as hostility towards their opponent or the mediator. "We're here to listen," they often say.

The more useful and successful strategy is to approach the mediation on the basis that it is a one-time all-out attempt to resolve the matter and not a stop along the way. "We want to be clear at the outset that we see today as our best chance of resolving this matter. We are approaching the mediation in that spirit. Any concessions granted today will be off the table, if we're unable to settle." If the other side knows that all bets are off at the end of the day, they will likely engage in a serious attempt to settle. In most cases, this will avoid the temptation to repeat offers made and rejected before the mediation. There is nothing wrong with referring to those efforts and explaining why you believed the offer was reasonable—if, indeed, it was.

Rather than regarding the mediator in this type of negotiation as the enemy, it makes a lot of sense to use the mediator to your advantage. Your first task is to build rapport with her and to build a bond of trust and understanding which provides you with a comfort level that assures you are involved in a fair process. Discuss your concerns openly in private meetings with the mediator and judge by the responses you receive.

Don't be in a hurry, especially in a case that is only about money. There is a delicate period at the beginning when everyone is feeling out the process and each other to achieve the desired mood, not unlike a first date.

> **TIP** The key to success in these mediations is to concentrate entirely on your own analysis, listening carefully for clues to those of your opponent. When you make a proposal, be prepared to give great detail to justify how and why you arrived at the number. Remember, you are being watched by your opponent and the mediator for signs of reasonableness. Be well aware that dismissively small or insulting concessions given early or repeating a previously rejected offer will send a strong negative message about your intentions.
>
> Recognizing early inescapable weaknesses, and acknowledging them while making a substantial concession, sends a positive message and invites reciprocity. If your opponent isn't prepared to respond in kind, you may calmly point that out and wait for more movement.
>
> Be prepared for a strong dose of reality from the mediator in these cases. Don't take this personally because the same thing is being done with your opponent. Work with the mediator and be real. You will be invited to justify your offer or counter-offer in the light of a number of realities, including the cost of litigation, your realistic chances of success, the time it will take to get to court and the cost of collecting, even if you are successful.
>
> If there remains a substantial gulf between you and your opponent, strive to understand why. There has to be a reason. If it's a good reason, you might well moderate your demands. If it's a bad one, you will have the opportunity to demonstrate the weakness and calmly invite them to reconsider.

LACK OF PREPARATION

Lack of preparation and unfamiliarity with the mediation process are the most common impediments to success. Parties or their lawyers who are ill-prepared do not, as a rule, participate actively. They tend to behave strategically in ways that are not productive, for example, by negotiating positionally. Positional negotiation takes very little preparation.

Not taking the mediation process seriously gives well-prepared opponents a tremendous advantage. Some of the strange wisdom I've overheard during the last three years include:

• "It's informal and you can make it up as you go along."

• "It's only a question of what's their bottom line and what's ours."

Lack of preparation may include failure to consult an expert, investigate the true facts, conduct a proper review of legal rights and appropriate remedies.

Mediation is consensual and getting an agreement is a process that requires cooperation from both sides to achieve agreement. It stands to reason that your chances of success improve immeasurably if both sides are well prepared because preparation is so central to achieving your goals in mediation. The following are important elements in preparing for mediation.

Understand Your Interests

Careful analysis of your own or the company's needs, concerns, and objectives will assist you in conveying to your lawyer and opponent what is important to you. Identify your essential basic interests, prioritize them, and evaluate their importance by assigning each a weight out of, say, a total of 100. When this analysis is complete, you will be able to articulate a range of acceptable options and time lines that reflect your priorities. You will also be in a position to seek the appropriate level of authority, if you do not possess it yourself.

Understand Their Interests

The same extensive analysis of your opponent's interests will further prepare you by helping you to evaluate realistically your position and the options you think might resolve all issues. What is important to them? Walk in their shoes. What are their suspected essential interests? Prioritize and evaluate them, assigning weights on the same basis.

Who Should Attend the Mediation?

Identify the key participants in the dispute. People who ought to be involved will be those who have a stake in the outcome. You must decide who will attend as part of your team and which of your lawyers will attend. Do you have the required authority? The fact that you have a pit bull on the case may be an asset in the courtroom but an overly aggressive counsel will be a liability at the mediation. Giving yourself every opportunity to resolve the matter should be your only consideration.

You send a message by who attends. For example, the attendance of the president or vice-president sends quite a different message than sending a junior human resources person. I am reminded of the old expression, "Don't send a boy on a man's job." Who should attend from the client perspective? Unlike court proceedings, in a mediation, the client, not the lawyer, is king. The client representative has a large role and is the senior partner at the mediation. Therefore, someone with obvious authority and complete knowledge of the issues is the ideal choice.

You should determine who you would like to have present from the other side and make your case to have them attend. If the attendance of someone is crucial to you, you may make their attendance a condition of proceeding. You definitely want someone who has the proper authority and is reasonably objective. For example, if a small business is operated by two partners, one whose expertise is technical, the other managerial, it would be unwise to send the technical partner to a mediation involving a dispute over a contract negotiated by the manager.

Consider Power, Cultural Differences, and Gender

Every dispute has unique dynamics based on the personalities of the parties and their representatives. Factors such as culture and gender should be carefully considered beforehand in order to avoid being surprised or committing unnecessary gaffes. For example, during a time of tension in the Middle East, an adjuster chosen to attend a mediation involving a claim by Hasidic Jews should probably not be a devout Muslim.

Anticipate Impasse or Deadlock

Having carefully reviewed your options, attempt to predict potential barriers and impasses. Review the material in this chapter and prepare your strategy. How will you handle barriers or deadlock? What will you say and how do you want to leave matters?

Prepare a Mediation Brief

You and your lawyer will prepare your mediation brief and provide your opponents with the arguments relating to each aspect of your case and any relevant documents such as reports, expert opinions, and copies of pertinent legal cases. There is no tactical advantage to suppressing relevant information, as we have seen. If you encounter reluctance or refusal to provide key information from your opponent's side, the chances of a successful mediation are slim. Several days before the mediation, you should meet again with your lawyer to discuss how your team will approach the mediation and your respective assignments.

The Law—It Is Important

Legal decisions that buttress your position are an important part of preparation for mediation in the context of a lawsuit. Failing to take the opportunity to expose weaknesses in your opponent's legal case in front of both client and lawyer is a golden opportunity missed. I have heard counsel say something to the effect that they will not presume to tell their learned friend the law. This is a complete cop-out, particularly because counsel usually believe their "learned friend" was asleep during most of the time at law school. In any event remember that it's for the client's ears since the client is the ultimate decision maker.

Role at the Table

You should decide who from your group will say what. What roles each of you will play is important. Careful thought to this task allocation will pay dividends. Is there any advantage in your saying certain things rather than your lawyer? Usually what you say carries a lot more weight with your opponent who will subconsciously discount your lawyer's pronouncements in the same way you will tend to discount theirs. This is the toll exacted by the adversarial process.

Bottom-line or strategic behaviour designed to get an edge will generally be seen as unprincipled. Some tactical behaviour—for example, good cop/bad cop—may be effective where your opponent's expectations are out of line with reality. Ask yourself what attitude you wish to present—cooperative, confident, indignant, indifferent, or apologetic?

Consider your attitudes and feelings towards your opponent. Review likely emotional issues and how you will cope with them. How will you react if provoked?

What is your walk-away position? Do you have one? Are you sufficiently flexible? Consider various acceptable and realistic options against the backdrop of your walk-away alternatives. You should have already considered what your walk-away position will be, namely, the point when you will be better off leaving the negotiation and taking your chances in court. What do you think is theirs? Can it be shifted?

☑ Preparation Checklist

❑ Do I understand the mediation process?

❑ Have I clearly analysed my interests—my concerns, needs, aspirations, fears?

❑ What are the other party's essential interests?

❑ What about cultural differences, gender issues, perspectives of power?

❑ What is our relationship with the other side? Now? Historically?

❑ Is our information complete?

❑ What do we need from them? Have we got it? If not, is mediation still worth pursuing without it, or do we need discovery first?

❑ Is our mediation brief complete? Is it readable, attractive, and simple? Will it be useful to have diagrams, plans, or charts? Are they ready?

❑ Is their anything in our mediation brief that is offensive? Is the tone closer to problem solving or blaming? Can the presentation be modified without altering the desired effect or facts?

- Is our theory of the case logical, simple, and compelling? If not, why not? Is it neutral in tone? If the dispute is technical, is there a glossary of terms?
- Is our investigation of all the facts complete?
- Are the witnesses and their statements credible?

❑ Has the law been properly and exhaustively researched? How important is it? Do we have reprints or excerpts?

❑ Do we have their mediation brief?

❑ Who should attend from our side? What about authority?

❑ Who do we want from their side?

❑ What will our roles be?

❑ What is our strategy if we reach impasse or deadlock? Where will it likely occur? Have we given enough thought to possible barriers and how to overcome them?

❑ Have we met with the mediator and signed the Agreement to Mediate?

DISCLOSURE OF INFORMATION

Negotiation is about sharing information. Complete information is needed to make intelligent decisions about whether or not to resolve a dispute. Barriers to resolution relating to information include:

- lack of important information, such as an expert medical report in a medical malpractice case; and
- failure or reluctance to exchange information freely, thus creating a distrustful, uncooperative climate which is not conducive to negotiation.

Getting Critical Information without Discoveries

While discoveries during litigation are the traditional method of obtaining information and very useful when used appropriately, conducting them unnecessarily may have serious consequences by way of further entrenching the parties, as we have seen. In most lawsuits the number of critical documents can be counted on the fingers of one or two hands. There may be two or three key witnesses and they are rarely needed in the mediation. Witness statements usually suffice. Experts' reports are required in most technical disputes. A good rule of thumb concerning experts' reports is, will they be needed at a trial for us to succeed? If so, they should be in hand and exchanged before the mediation.

How key information is identified and shared before mediation is a critical question in preparing for a productive session.

Your Information

All documents and files should be organized in a logical, perhaps chronological, order. Any persons having information bearing on the dispute should be identified, and interviewed, and their statements obtained. Objective data should be identified and obtained as early as possible. For example, in cases of professional negligence (such as medical, legal, engineering, or architectural malpractice), a report from a respected expert identifying the specifics of the negligence must be obtained before the mediation. When your documentary and factual preparation is completed, it should be organized to support your arguments. During this process, documents and information in the possession of others will be identified, and you are then in a position to ask for them.

Their Information

If litigation has already been started, allegations have been made and they will have to be supported.

TIP In preparing for mediation, assuming you have decided to try to avoid discovery, you will simply ask for the material that is relevant to support the contentions of the other side. It is better to ask specifically for what you want, than simply to say "give me everything you have." However, in order to catch material you are not aware of, this type of general request may also be necessary.

It is often very useful at some early stage in the dispute to sit down with your opponent to flesh out what is needed on both sides. Sometimes this may occur lawyer to lawyer, with or without the client present. The meeting will give you an opportunity to establish some personal rapport, as well to assess your opponent, her style and demeanour.

DIFFICULT PEOPLE

Difficult people have been the topic of many books and articles, and may include your opponents, their lawyer, your lawyer, the mediator, and even you. You take people as you find them. Some display irksome behaviour because they are nervous. They may not even know they are annoying you. They may be quick tongued or sarcastic or have irritating ticks. It really shouldn't matter. The best advice that I can give is that unfailing courtesy goes a long way. If these activities are intentional, but obviously missing their mark, they will end. Also keep your eye on the ball, your ball, so that you are not diverted from your course. Remember, you only have to deal with it until the mediation is over.

TIP My rule about treating your opponents as you would your grandparents, (who, like all of us, are not without foibles), may work for you. If you demonstrate courtesy towards your opponents, the mediator, and the process, you will be amazed at how this will defuse difficult people. The courtesy may be returned in kind. Concentrate on solving the problems, not on your opponents' personality.

DIFFICULT BEHAVIOUR

Difficult behaviour is behaviour that, by design, has the potential to derail the mediation. Included are such things as put-downs, interruptions, slamming briefcases or books, and any behaviour that suggests lack of common courtesy such as sighs, grunts, turning away, twirling pens, rolling eyes, or flipping through files. Calling someone a liar, cheat, or fraud; criticizing; diagnosing; name-calling and sarcasm; ordering; ingratiating praise; moralizing; advising; diverting; inappropriate questions; appealing to somebody's sense of logic; finishing people's sentences; and second-guessing motives are also examples of difficult behaviour.

Dishonesty, misinformation, insupportable demands, threats, trickery, or sleazy negotiating tactics such as the never-ending ratcheting up of demands, last-minute "add ons," for instance, and "we'll also need to be reimbursed for the research and development costs," are other examples of difficult behaviour.

Tough-minded or hard-nosed negotiation is not difficult behaviour provided it is based in reality. Unwillingness to compromise essential interests is principled behaviour, not difficult behaviour. Even mild emotion such as exasperation, impatience, annoyance, indignation, and irritability are acceptable and may be used to good effect. Mediation is not an elegant dance like a minuet or gavotte; it is an event that may sometimes feel like a full-contact sport.

As we have seen in Chapter 4, your lawyer can make a vital contribution to the success of the mediation. However, there are a few lawyers who put their own pecuniary interest above the interests of their clients and as such, they are in serious conflict of interest. It is not generally difficult to tell if you are dealing with these types of lawyers. They tend to attack the mediator in the same way a dog attacks someone trying to take away its favourite bone.

The lawyer who says "we are going to win this case" and who does not concede the possibility of losing, is of little assistance. While most lawyers take their roles as officers of the court seriously, there is a minority who are too closely involved in their clients' case, and lose their objectivity. Your lawyer should be able to provide you with a realistic assessment of the likelihood of success and failure at a trial. Your lawyer's main contribution in any mediation is to predict the probable outcome of a trial and reassess that prediction periodically during the course of the negotiation, as new information emerges.

Lawyers who act towards one another in a rude and deprecating manner do not assist the process, nor do they bring credit to their profession.

TIP Unacceptable and difficult behaviour suggests discomfort with the process or perhaps a weak case on the merits. At some level, it is calculated to overthrow the mediation. Be persistent. Don't allow somebody who is using these tactics to get under your skin if the mediator is not doing anything about it. Consider calling them on their behaviour or at least asking whether or not the behaviour is intended to frustrate the negotiation.

Nothing succeeds better than shining light on inappropriate behaviour. Speak to the mediator about it. If it persists after the mediator has called attention to it, you have a decision to make. Your only option, if it still persists and becomes intolerable, may be to disengage from the process temporarily, or permanently.

BAD TIMING

Attempting mediation after a dispute has languished for some months or years is less likely to produce success for several reasons. Considerable time and money may have been invested in the winner-take-all process of litigation. As time and money are expended, negative emotions increase and goodwill decreases as the parties become more entrenched.

Justice delayed is truly justice denied. For example, if an insurance company assigns a reserve (the amount insurance companies are required by law to set aside for the settlement of claims) of $20,000 to a personal injury claim, and the cost of the independent medical examination, coupled with legal defence costs after a three-day discovery, totals $6,000 before the mediation, there will be $12,000 left for the plaintiff. If the plaintiff's legal fees are also $8,000, there is only $4,000 for the plaintiff. What is wrong with this picture?

The further down the litigation road the parties have travelled emotionally and financially and the closer they are to winning (they don't like to think too much about losing), the less disposed they will be to working out an agreement that suits them both.

If discoveries are needed, as they may well be, it is very important to get on with them as soon as possible and to conduct them in a manner that leaves the parties not too much the worse for wear. This will pay huge dividends later when the mediation does takes place.

TIP Require your lawyer to provide you with a closely reasoned written opinion on the legal merits of your case, both pro and con, early in the process. The opinion will be without the benefit of discoveries but well worth it.

It is understandable why lawyers want to have discoveries. Discoveries are a way of turning over and examining meticulously every rock, nook, and cranny of the dispute. It is important to do that if your working assumption is that you are going to a trial. In such a case you want your lawyer to be very thorough to avoid losing. But remember, 95% of cases settle before trial.

By getting a detailed written early assessment of your case, you will be able to understand clearly your walk-away position, an essential to successful mediation. Should the mediation fail, you can still proceed with discoveries.

UNREALISTIC EXPECTATIONS

Unrealistically high expectations of parties or their lawyers may be the single most difficult barrier in mediation. We expect our lawyers to sound confident and aggressive in court or, for that matter, in public, but if we do not encourage them to provide realistic advice concerning our downside risks for the purposes of negotiation, we are doing ourselves a tremendous disservice.

Overly optimistic, early assessments of the strengths of a case present difficulties. Intemperate language, sometimes used by lawyers in describing their opponent's case, such as "vexatious and completely without merit" and "totally lacking credibility" are hard to back away from. Immoderate language is one of the worst aspects of the adversarial system where lawyers are bound to put the best face on even bad cases, highlighting the strengths and minimizing the weaknesses in the usually faint hope that their opponents and the judges will overlook them. Usually the posturing moderates considerably as the trial approaches and the likelihood of losing looms large.

Principled negotiation depends on both sides assessing their cases realistically. This task should not be left to the mediator. If the mediation begins with one side saying black and the other white, I know we are in for a long day.

> **TIP** In preparing for mediation, assume your opponent will have unrealistic expectations and an inflated view of their chances of success in court. The mediation is a golden opportunity to deflate those expectations by gently probing areas that are unsubstantiated, questioning underlying assumptions, and providing neutral data to demonstrate weaknesses. Where possible, use objective yardsticks so you will both feel you are dealing with the problem fairly.
>
> At the same time examine your own expectations under a microscope. Think about your alternatives if you fail to reach agreement. What will you really do and what are the true financial, human, and lost costs that you will face?

MISSING PARTY

Before mediating, a careful review of who should logically be at the table is crucial to success. There is nothing worse than having to agree an hour or less into a mediation that without so-and-so, there really isn't any point in proceeding. Intricate multiparty-issue disputes are particularly susceptible to this problem because it is more difficult to know who should be at the table from the outset. However, the same thing can happen in simple cases if care isn't taken when the mediation is being set up.

In our complex society, one hears more and more, "It wasn't my fault, it was theirs" or "We hired them to do the job, they gave a warranty, it's their responsibility." This happens all the time in construction cases where there are multiple layers of responsibility between consultants, contractor, subcontractors, and the owner. We have seen that in the simple mall fall everyone was pointing the finger at somebody else. The same thing can happen in a multiple car accident or a case of medical malpractice where several doctors, nurses, and the hospital are involved.

> **TIP** When agreeing to mediate make sure you carefully review whether all parties who must participate in any agreement to resolve the matter have been identified. I am not talking about all witnesses or even experts who have provided reports, rather key players whose interests are affected by the dispute. Known parties should be questioned about whether they think someone else should be at the table to share responsibility.

OVEREMPHASIS ON SETTLEMENT

A mediator who ruthlessly pushes for settlement knowing that an agreement may not be in the best interests of one of the parties, is acting unprofessionally and may just get everyone's back up. Mediators must not have a stake in any outcome at all. Their province is ensuring a productive process. Too much emphasis on settlement rates by mediators is inappropriate. Obviously, mediators who are not effective, who aren't able to achieve results, will not be in great demand, but there is a big difference between overemphasis and no emphasis.

TIP Choose a mediator who will help you achieve your goals. People want to resolve their disputes and expect the mediator to work hard to achieve their objective. This usually means the mediator will take a very active role during the mediation. But it does not mean being pushy or coercive and telling the parties what to do and how to do it, or that their "settlement rate" is in jeopardy because the parties cannot agree.

CULTURAL BARRIERS

Since negotiation and mediation require a high level of communication, if there are language difficulties or a major cultural gulf between the parties, the mediator will have to decide whether or not they can be overcome creatively.

When the problem is language, using interpreters may be a solution. A relative may or may not be appropriate depending on their skill as an interpreter and concerns about accuracy. The relative must not act as a filter and distort the communications between the parties. A professional interpreter is preferable.

Likewise, in a cross-cultural dispute, attention must be paid to whether the necessary sensitivity to the cultural differences between the parties will be possible and whether, in fact, they will understand each other. Similarly, will the mediator understand when cultural differences may distort understanding. For example, in mediations involving aboriginal land claims between First Nations peoples and the government, it may be appropriate to use a "cultural interpreter" or a co-mediator capable of ensuring that the desired level of understanding is achieved. By using a co-mediator model, concerns about bias may also be assuaged.

POWER IMBALANCES

This important subject, first mentioned in Chapter 1, is discussed extensively in mediation literature. Some writers suggest that a mediator may be able to shift the balance of power where an inequity exists—indeed, that the mediator has a responsibility in this regard. If power is being abused, a private chat by the mediator may result in changed behaviour. Just as important may be an attempt to deal with the other side's feelings of powerlessness. Cases involving power imbalance are, for example, negotiating with a bank that has called your line of credit, an insurance company who refuses to pay your claim, or a small business negotiating with Revenue Canada about GST allegedly owing.

While you may be able to teach a 300-pound gorilla to dance, if you dance too closely, the gorilla will step on your toes. No mediator I know can make a 300-pound gorilla lose 200 pounds or teach it to waltz, nor should they. The fact is there are 300-pound gorillas in the real world. While a mediator may provide some negotiation "coaching" to participants in a mediation, the best protection from abuse of power is preparation and negotiation skill. There is no substitute for knowing your walk-away position and being able to conduct a principled, articulate negotiation.

A mediator who is obviously attempting to shift power is on very thin ice indeed, possibly verging on compromising her neutrality. If you are feeling leaned upon unduly or pressured, or detect signs of bias during a mediation, you should question the mediator about his views relating to power imbalances. Life does not deal out equal power to all parties in a negotiation. You have to take power as it is dealt and do your best to even the playing field. Litigation is hardly equal. Parties have unequal resources and time pressures. Counsel are rarely equal in experience, knowledge, or ability.

While we can encourage people to engage in principled negotiation, we cannot force them to. Strategic use of power tactics—delay, for example, by those who can better afford delay—is not illegal. The best protection against an abuse of power, or when you discover someone is not negotiating in good faith, is to proceed directly to court. Our courts are charged with the responsibility of meting out justice even though justice can sometimes be blind.

Sometimes parties perceive negotiation to be against their better interests, perhaps because they are uncertain of their ability to negotiate or perceive that somehow "compromise" may be morally or politically wrong. Some women's groups have put forward concerns about mediating family disputes or abuse cases. They argue women are placed at a disadvantage in negotiations. Similarly, small investors and business people recoil from mediating disputes with banks and investment dealers. These factors must be carefully considered before undertaking mediation and weighed against the alternatives in an imperfect world.

TIP   The problem may be corrected through process design. For example, the concern may relate to a practice in family mediations of not having lawyers present or shuttling between parties where anger and volatility have escalated and the parties haven't yet acquired the skills to communicate face to face.

The alternatives, such as going to court may be even less attractive.

LACK OF RESOURCES

In any mediation, you have to consider realistically the resources that are available. If you hear "your demands are totally outrageous. I'm better off taking my chances in court, where anything can happen." Translation: "I don't have the money to pay if I lose." During several mediations, either voluntarily or prompted by me, defendants have said they were seriously considering bankruptcy because of lack of resources.

Pursuing a lawsuit to judgement, only to find that the prospects of collecting are nil, is not good business. Through negotiation, creative ways and means may be found to avoid this outcome, as well as to test the validity of a poverty claim. Pursuing these claims may result in obtaining a judgement— a piece of paper which is worth nothing. Remember, lawyers or judges don't guarantee payment. The cost of collecting on a judgement can be staggering even after a successful trial. Worse yet, the loser may have placed their assets beyond your reach or be tapped out by the time you get a judgement. A lawsuit can take one to four years, and that doesn't include an appeal.

TIP   If your dispute is about money, be sure to do some independent research beforehand to determine your opponent's ability to pay. Be prepared to be flexible if payment is a problem by agreeing to terms that your opponent can meet. In one case, a party agreed to give an affidavit under oath listing all assets and liabilities, to supply his last three years' income tax returns and to submit to a cross-examination of these documents if required. With this, the claimant was willing to take much less than she expected because there was an objective way of checking the validity of the claim of limited resources. Parties who ignore reality, who cannot accept less than a full loaf, often end up with crumbs.

INSTITUTIONAL BARRIERS

Some mediations have built-in, difficult-to-detect barriers. Not unlike computer viruses, they lurk beneath the surface.

Corporate politics may sometimes dictate that the matter in dispute be tossed like a hot potato to counsel who will then have to shoulder the blame, along with the judge, if the case is lost. With any luck, it will take several years to get to trial and memories will be dim, or the responsible parties will have moved on up the corporate ladder. But the company's shareholders and society in general pay a price for this irresponsible shell game in the form of lower profits or higher prices. Many companies are recognizing the high cost of unresolved disputes and are rewarding behaviour that removes them from the books early.

TIP When dealing in a mediation with any large bureaucracy, whether corporate or governmental, spend time at the beginning understanding the approvals process and level of authority possessed by the individual negotiator. Will any agreement have to be ratified by the board of directors, a senior officer, or the municipal council? If an agreement is reached, will the negotiator strongly recommend acceptance? How much weight will that carry? If the authority is limited, make certain that it is limited to "reasonable" parameters.

Spend some time getting a feel for their intention to negotiate or "zeal for the deal," as I have heard it described. If they say they are there to "listen," you will have your answer.

Inflexible or inadequate authority based on unrealistic assessments or erroneous perceptions will shackle the negotiators and cause impasse. Flexibility is critical because erroneous perceptions or misunderstandings are frequently clarified during the mediation. For example, municipal councils may incur high litigation costs rather than bite the bullet and make the tough decisions they are elected to make, thus increasing the tax burden on the long-suffering voter.

WHAT IF THE MEDIATION BECOMES DEADLOCKED?

While some tips to overcoming barriers were provided under their respective headings, there remains the question of what to do if the mediation bogs down and becomes deadlocked. This can happen. People run out of steam. They believe they have reached their walk-way position. In other words, they like their alternatives better than what is on the table. You should rely on the mediator and his persistence to overcome impasse. Some of the things the mediator might do include:

- reviewing and questioning privately each party's walk-away position and using reality checks, questions, or objective data to shift these positions;
- reviewing and summarizing the progress already made, which serves to refocus everybody's attention on their objectives and may provide a note of optimism at the right time;
- attempting to create a climate that will generate additional ways of breaking the logjam;
- moving to less difficult issues as progress is made to increase everyone's investment in the process;
- suggesting objective standards or experts on which both sides agree;
- offering creative suggestions which are not owned by either side (either side will feel free to attack, endorse, or modify such suggestions without worrying about offending the other side);
- reviewing available process options, including another session if more homework is required to develop better information, suggesting another mediator, or possibly even arbitration or another ADR process.

TIP While these are some of the things the mediator might do, she will need your help. To some extent, the mediator is an empty vessel that requires filling by you. For example, you might suggest a reality-check question or provide the objective data needed to reduce unrealistic expectations. Rather than coming from you, it is sanitized coming from the mediator. This is perfectly acceptable, so long as the information is accurate and complete.

Perhaps the most powerful technique is creating a positive climate and demonstrating persistence and a strong commitment to overcoming difficulties as they are encountered.

 # AGREEMENT

GETTING THERE

There comes a time in every mediation when everything has been said and all necessary information has been tabled and examined. A picture has emerged not only of each party's position but of what the dispute is really about, and everyone knows what items each party thinks are important. There may be no way to know at this stage the precise importance that should be placed on those items. Their existence should, however, be known and the broad terms to be included or addressed in any agreement should have been discussed.

CLOSURE

The time has now arrived for everybody to roll up their sleeves, review each proposal, and compare options against their walk-away positions. This is the time for the "rubber to hit the road." There is no room for posturing at this stage. If either party is too demanding or fails to properly assess the minimum needs of their adversaries, the mediation may end abruptly. This is a time for moderation and flexibility.

SEPARATE PROPOSALS OR OFFERS

I often challenge both sides to prepare proposals that they believe may resolve the matter and be acceptable to the other side. I will then visit with both sides separately, to refine these proposals. If certain needs or concerns of either side remain unaddressed, I point these out to permit further refinements.

SINGLE-TEXT AGREEMENT

I ask both sides which one would like to present its proposal first and I may provide some coaching on how the proposal should be presented or what might be said in support of the various components of the package. Where the parties are well along in their discussions of options and working together (the ideal situation, but not always achieved in a three-to-five-hour session involving highly emotional and polarized disputants), I will work with the parties jointly to develop a single-text agreement, reviewing all options and refining them until a satisfactory agreement emerges.

WHO MAKES THE FIRST MOVE?

Some negotiators are loath to make the first offer. You hear such excuses as "I'm the plaintiff, my claim is my first offer" or "they're the plaintiff, they should know what they want." While there may be some risks associated with making the first offer such as reactive devaluation (the tendency to dismiss as insubstantial because *it is in hand*), the order of who pitches and who catches is, more often than not, immaterial. In some cases, if the perceived risks of going first are too high, it may make sense to have the mediator "float" a proposal as his own and have the parties work from it as a single text until it meets with unanimous approval.

During this last phase of the mediation, the parties will have to confront their alternatives and walk-away positions realistically when weighing various options to see how they stack up. If you are able to say in good conscience, after consulting everyone on your team, that you will definitely be better off rejecting all options and walking away, fine. The more usual scenario is to reject certain options and concentrate on others, in which case you will be nearing agreement.

MOMENTUM

Strong momentum occurs in the final phases of most negotiations. If everyone has been working hard to find a solution, it may be risky to delay agreement until another day in the hope of improving the deal. The best time for reaching an agreement is while everyone is at the table and "in the moment." It is human nature to agonize over and devalue what is in hand. In a litigious context, however, a bird in the hand, is more often than not, truly worth two in the bush. Remember, everyone at the table will experience the same feelings of dissapointment if talks are broken off without achieving agreement. I am not advocating entering into poorly analysed or improvident agreements. However, there is a time to seize the moment. If the moment is missed, the deal may go cold. Experienced negotiators and mediators know this and apply a little pressure at these moments. If the deal is better than you are likely to achieve if you walk away, don't resist.

SETTLEMENT REMORSE

Bottom-line negotiators find the closing minutes of the mediation horribly agonizing. They worry that "we may have left something on the table." They are always second-guessing themselves because negotiation, for them, is about getting all that you can. Principled negotiators will know whether the proposed agreement meets their objectives based on their walk-away position.

HALLMARKS OF A GOOD AGREEMENT

A good agreement must be efficient, fair, durable, and enforceable. Without these characteristics, it will fall apart in short order. If the agreement is not efficient, items excluded will pop up later and cause problems; if it is not enforceable, the agreement is worse than useless, and will not stand the test of time. It is but a stopgap measure.

All prospective agreements should be reviewed against these criteria and if found wanting, they should be amended.

TESTING THE AGREEMENT

Issue by issue, the agreement should be tested against the following criteria.

Efficient

Does the agreement address all parties' identified interests? You will have taken considerable pains to identify your interests if you followed the guidelines in Chapter 5 while preparing for the mediation. Does the proposed agreement address them? Will the agreement wash with everyone you answer to—your boss, the senior claims manager, the board of directors, your family, or associates? What resources will be consumed in complying with the agreement? What emotional resources will be required? Will compliance with the agreement use up more resources than the alternatives to entering into the agreement (your walk-away position)? If problems are identified in these areas, now is the time to amend the agreement.

Fair

Fairness is perhaps the most elusive and important quality of any agreement. What we think of as fair will depend on who we are, our values, background, culture, and psychological make up. How has the dispute affected us, our interests, and emotions? Clearly the impact of the dispute on us will likely be very different than it is for the other side. No one's reaction, whether corporately or personally, to a conflict are exactly mirrored by those of their opponent.

Understanding this vital fact during negotiations and while evaluating an agreement is essential to achieving success. Ways and means must be found to apply objective, valid criteria to the agreement that both sides agree upon. Too often instead of making the effort to support proposed alternatives with uncontested objective data, parties argue needlessly about the "obvious" fairness of their proposals or take the lazy way out and propose that someone else, for example, a judge or ex-judge, be consulted.

Durable

Look to the future. Visualize the effects of implementing the terms of the agreement. Consider the other side, the people you answer to, your organization's policies, your family, your suppliers, and competitors. Imagine all possible contingencies. Will adjustments have to be made in these relationships? Are they workable? If not, the agreement will not stand the test of time.

Enforceable

Is the agreement enforceable? Elegant agreements that fail the legal test, and therefore are unenforceable, are useless. If solutions contravene competition, family, or tax laws, the hard work of the mediation will be to no avail. This is a good reason to have your lawyer present at the mediation, particularly if the mediation is about an existing or contemplated lawsuit.

When legal issues are involved, your lawyer must be present. If the matters in dispute are before the courts because litigation has been commenced, it will be important for the lawyers to be involved throughout the mediation.

If the parties have identified the issues in dispute and are mediating to avoid litigation, judgement in using lawyers will have to be exercised.

Certainly they must be involved in vetting any agreement with legal implications and will be of assistance in assuring what you have agreed is covered by the written document. In complex business, estate, and family matters, lawyers should be involved throughout as needed.

THE AGREEMENT—TIPS FOR GETTING A GOOD AGREEMENT

Write It Up

When everything is settled, a draft agreement should be prepared. It is important to do this while the agreement is still fresh. It also helps to identify any problems and resolve them before settlement remorse has a chance to work its magic.

Never agree to "let the lawyers go back to their office and exchange agreements." There are too many stories about that process taking six months or more. There are also stories of further disputes erupting or a genuine disagreement about the agreed terms. Resist the temptation to "leave it to the lawyers." This is a natural inclination in the euphoria and exhaustion that often accompanies the end of difficult negotiations.

The preferable course is to complete a full draft agreement and refine it to the point where it is complete and can be properly executed. This ensures all points have been understood and agreed. There is also time for sober second thought and an opportunity to apply the tests referred to earlier: efficiency, fairness, durability, and enforceability. This testing will uncover flaws which might otherwise torpedo or delay implementation of the agreement.

Even in the most straightforward dispute, writing out the points of agreement and dealing with how issues will be dealt with in future will assist the parties to follow up appropriately.

The Agreement Is Public Unless Otherwise Stated

Unless the agreement contains provisions to the effect that the terms of the agreement are confidential, the document can be made public. The agreement is not governed by the confidentiality provisions agreed to during the mediation. The parties intend to be bound by it and therefore must intend the agreement to be public.

If You Want It to Be Confidential, Say So

It is not uncommon for these agreements to contain a provision that maintains confidentiality and it may even provide for penalties if the confidence is breached. Such agreements contain exceptions in the event of a breach or for disclosure to government authorities with jurisdiction and for disclosure to personal or corporate advisors such as lawyers or accountants.

Remember, It Is the Parties' Agreement

Whenever possible, the parties' own words and plain English should be used rather than legalese. You should insist on this unless there are very convincing reasons advanced to the contrary, for example, where such phraseology is important from a legal or technical perspective. Not only are plain English agreements in vogue, far more importantly, you—not the lawyers—will have to live with and abide by the agreement.

Tie Down All Loose Ends

During this final phase as the various points are dealt with, I find myself asking all kinds of questions. Who will do that? By when? When will the payment be made? What happens if it isn't? Will there be a grace period? Are there any tax implications? Does this agreement have to be ratified by the board? Perhaps the most important question is: what will be the consequences of not abiding by the agreement? These questions should all be answered in the agreement.

Use the Mediator

When taking the time to hash out a detailed agreement, important and difficult questions inevitably emerge. There are often differences of opinion about implementation or the details of what was agreed upon. This is the time when the mediator is invaluable. The parties have placed their trust in him and will usually permit the mediator considerable latitude in making suggestions to bridge these last-minute glitches.

Consider using the mediator as the supervisor of the implementation of the settlement terms. Using the mediator as a stakeholder or final arbiter in the case of minor disagreements may work wonders. For example, the parties may have agreed to submit certain questions to an accountant or engineer of their own choosing. Should they not be able to agree on who that should be, they might entrust the selection to the mediator.

Don't Use the Mediator to Draft the Agreement

If the lawyers have been involved from the beginning, they are best qualified to draft the agreement, with assistance from the mediator if haggling over details becomes a problem. Avoid having the mediator involved in drafting the agreement if the lawyers have been involved, unless it is absolutely necessary. While the agreement will be neutral in tone, there may be problems with interpretation which would put the mediator in the awkward position of having to be a witness at any subsequent court case.

Use a Dispute Resolution Clause

The key to resolving disputes and avoiding them in the future will be how carefully the parties address issues of follow-up and implementation. But, there will always be unanticipated contingencies. In more complicated multiparty, multiissue disputes which require the agreement to be implemented over time, you should anticipate disputes arising from the agreement and provide a built-in means of resolution by including a dispute resolution clause. At a minimum, any dispute resolution clause should include direct negotiations between the parties as a first step, followed by the appointment of a pre-selected mediator if the matter is unresolved after a stipulated time period. If a mediated resolution is not achieved, arbitration should be considered.

Does the Agreement End the Dispute?

The agreement should end the dispute for all time, if possible. Releases and waivers should be part of any agreement.

WHEN IT'S OVER, IT'S OVER!

It is very important at the end of a dispute for the parties to symbolically let go and celebrate their good work. Signing an agreement and shaking hands has an important place in any negotiation. Shaking hands, even if agreement hasn't been reached, sets an appropriate tone for continued discussions.

WHAT HAPPENS IF THE AGREEMENT IS BROKEN?

People who attend mediations that result in agreement want to know what happens if the other side doesn't live up to the deal. Is the agreement as good as a court judgement? Any agreement is only as good as its contents. It may be much better than a court judgement or not worth the paper it is written on. That is why it is so important to get legal advice before signing any agreement and preferably to help prepare it.

The reasons a mediated agreement is potentially more valuable than a court judgement are:

- The agreement might provide that a court judgement be consented to by one of the parties to be held by the other in abeyance so long as the provisions of the agreement are observed. In the event of a failure to abide by the terms, for example, non-payment of money on the agreed date, the party holding the judgement could proceed to enforce it in the same manner as you would a court judgement (i.e., by employing bailiffs or the sheriff to seize and sell the defaulting party's property).

- The agreement may be as rich as the imaginations of the parties. It may provide for things a court would never order. For example, it may require that security be posted in the event of a breach, for an escalation of payments, or even a penalty.

- The agreement is a contract that distils the parties' preferred options and narrows the dispute to manageable proportions. This is very significant compared to what existed at the beginning of the mediation. If the contract is broken, quite apart from security, escalations, or penalties, it is a much more succinct document which sets out each person's rights and obligations, making it much easier to enforce.

NON-AGREEMENT

Inevitably, a small number of mediations will end without agreement on some or even all of the issues. There are a number of important things to remember if this happens. You will be upset, disappointed, and frustrated since a tremendous amount of time, effort, money, and high expectations have been invested in achieving an end to the dispute.

Some points to bear in mind are:

• Take time to carefully review all the issues and clearly state where the problems lie for you. In doing so, you invite further dialogue which can sometimes overcome the difficulty. In any event, no one should leave without a very well-defined understanding of the areas of non-agreement and the options available for resolution.

• Consider the mediation as an event in the life of the dispute. Undoubtedly, throughout the process, insight as to where each of the disputants is coming from will have been gained. It may be that more information needs to be developed or that the timing was not right. Leave the door open for further discussions, either directly or by agreeing to a further mediation.

• Consider asking the mediator for an evaluation or advisory opinion on the outstanding issues, provided the mediator has the necessary background. In certain cases, this approach may help the parties bridge the gap but should only be used as a last-ditch effort.

• Feel free to find common ground with your opponents by blaming the mediator's shortcomings for the lack of closure. Consider retaining another mediator if the prospects are reasonable that a fresh approach might succeed. Good mediators will not take this personally. They will appreciate the value of new approaches and the importance of saving face.

• Remember, only that particular mediation session or series of sessions is over. The dispute remains. Don't burn your bridges by leaving in a huff or accusing your opponent of negotiating in bad faith. Be gracious and agree to continue your efforts to resolve the matter. Remember, over 95% of disputes settle before a trial.

• Discuss whether other ADR options might resolve the matter rather than commencing or continuing with a lawsuit.

• If you decide to proceed with the litigation or an arbitration, use the opportunity afforded by the mediation to discuss ground rules to avoid further conflict. Are there ways to move things along quickly? What are the areas of agreement? How can expense be reduced?

7

ALL DISPUTES
ARE NOT
THE SAME

This chapter examines a number of different types or classes of disputes with the object of highlighting their unique characteristics. These differences may influence the timing or approach of the parties and the mediator to the dispute. Just as disputants differ in personality, the same is true of conflict. The type of resolution sought also differs. The beauty of mediation is that it can be designed to meet the specific needs of any dispute. One type of dispute may require more fact finding or discovery than another. In some disputes the level of distrust and dislike may be so high that until small steps are taken to build a bridge or foundation for more ambitious steps, face-to-face meetings may be absolutely counter-productive. This is particularly true in some family disputes, sexual harassment, abuse, or incest cases. Flexibility of design, technique, and the style applied by the mediator may vary widely to respond best to the requirements of the conflict. This is the singular strength of mediation.

In the following sections I have attempted to isolate some of these factors to better assist you in succeeding with mediation, no matter which type of dispute you may be involved in. The case studies are based on fact but in order to preserve confidentiality, they are composites of many cases mediated by me over the past three years.

COMMERICAL CASES

Commercial cases, particularly these days, require early and effective resolution since a business relationship will rarely survive the litigation process. A dispute between supplier and manufacturer, or the shareholders, directors, or officers of a company should not be allowed to languish for years in the courts if the company is to thrive. Because business is such a dynamic process, it is extremely sensitive to the passage of time, costs of litigation, and perhaps most important, uncertainty. It is precisely because business is adverse to risk that whenever possible, alternatives to litigation should be explored.

Process Design

In complex commercial cases the design and structure of the mediation process should be tailored to the nature of the dispute, the number of parties involved, and their representatives. Whether or not the decision makers will be present, whether experts are needed, a workable timetable and logical agenda are all important ingredients to successful commercial mediation.

A mediator with a commercial background should be chosen in order to minimize the time required to "educate" him. Consideration should be given to using co-mediators if the issues are very complex and there are more than four or five parties. Co-mediation is particularly useful when the issues are highly technical, for example, patents or trade marks, engineering of complex manufacturing equipment or processes, and multilayered securities cases. In these cases it may be useful to select, as one of the mediators, a person who possesses unquestioned expertise. Alternatively, the parties may, by agreement, designate an expert who will assist the mediator as needed. Preparation and exchange of necessary information on a timely basis is also critical to successfully mediating commercial cases.

The ground rules of proceeding should be settled well in advance including whether the parties wish the mediator to act as an arbitrator in the case of impasse. A detailed agreement to mediate which sets out the location and requirements for technology, overheads, teleconferencing, and fax will pay large dividends.

The mediator should meet the decision makers to ensure their understanding of, and support for, the process. Ideally, they will be present themselves or provide their negotiators with suitable flexible authority. Commercial disputes are often characterized by mounds of information and documents and may involve numerous parties in multiple locations. The mediator must work with the parties to design a process which minimizes the amount of disruption for the parties' organizations while making sure information relevant to the negotiation is available.

Arbitration is seen by many as useful in resolving commercial disputes and it has become particularly popular in the United States, where it appears more frequently in contracts. It is not uncommon in commercial agreements to see several pages of contract devoted to outlining the procedures for selecting the arbitrator and the ground rules that will govern the proceedings.

Caution should be exercised before deciding to arbitrate as a first step in commercial cases. It is worth noting that the growth of arbitration is an American response to problems that do not exist in Canada:

• Canadian juries are notoriously stingy compared to their American counterparts and American companies seek to avoid outlandish awards by requiring that their disputes be arbitrated.

• There is little incentive to settle in those American states which permit contingency fees, whereby the lawyer shares in the proceeds of the litigation to the tune of 30% or 40%. Contingency fees foster a bonanza mentality, often prompting claimants to "shoot for the moon" rather than settle for a reasonable amount.

• There are considerably greater difficulties in getting a case to trial in many states than in Canada.

• The level of confidence in our judicial system and judiciary is higher than in the United States.

TIP Arbitration may be useful in certain highly technical disputes or to overcome impasse if mediation fails. Mediation should, however, be attempted as a first step in most cases. It's cheaper, faster, and less cumbersome. When successful, it results in a negotiated agreement that satisfies both sides. In arbitration, one party loses.

Case Study

Two partners had a falling out over the promotion and development of certain products created by processes to which they owned the patents jointly. One of the partners, the inventor, had considerable scientific expertise, having created the processes and patented them. The other partner had business acumen and access to the capital necessary to develop the products and bring them into production.

The relationship between the partners was governed by several agreements which required that any dispute between them must be arbitrated. No rules of procedure for the arbitration were, however, set out in the agreement. The agreements also provided that the inventor convey the patents to a jointly controlled company.

The dispute arose over whether or not to grant an exclusive licence for North America to an American company in exchange for royalty payments. The inventor favoured this course but the businessman thought the deal was bad and was sure another company could be found. Negotiations commenced and bogged down. Both partners refused to budge. The inventor had not yet transferred the patents to the jointly controlled company. Meanwhile, the very existence of the patents became threatened by the passage of time.

The businessman, fearing stalemate would further jeopardize the valuable patents, commenced an involved legal action urgently requesting that the inventor partner be prevented from dealing with the patents and that the patents be conveyed to a company jointly owned by the disputing parties.

During the court-ordered mediation it became evident that:

- The partners would continue to be entangled by the agreements even if the court ordered the patents conveyed to a jointly-owned company. The real impasse between them, namely who would finance and develop the patents, would remain unaddressed.

- Both parties realized that the two or three years it would take to litigate the matter would result in the competition getting the jump on them and the opportunity might be lost or seriously diminished.

- Each party respected the other's expertise and needed what the other had, but they couldn't work together as equal partners.

- Proceeding to arbitrate so many issues would be time-consuming and expensive.

- One of the partners had the technical knowledge and no money or business sense to properly develop the products, while the other had both the money and development expertise but not the technical know-how.

Once the cards were on the table, the partners worked towards achieving a workable arrangement which provided the inventor with the assurances he required that development of his inventions would move forward, compensation during the development period would be escalated over time and if payments weren't made, the rights to the patents would be reverted to the inventor.

The financial partner received an exclusive licence to develop the patents unimpeded by the inventor who would, as needed, supply technical advice so long as the minimum royalty was paid. Upon development, royalty revenue would be shared equally after an appropriate adjustment for prepaid royalties. This agreement was achieved in a four-hour mediation following several months of stalemate and litigation.

PERSONAL INJURY CLAIMS

Personal injury claims are being successfully mediated throughout North America. They possess unique characteristics which present special challenges and opportunities in mediation. In Ontario, personal injury claims resulting from motor vehicle accidents are mediated at the Ontario Insurance Commission. Ontario recently passed legislation enhancing the rights of motorists to sue for personal injuries sustained in a car accident. Workers' Compensation legislation in Ontario now makes mediation mandatory.

Personal injury cases include not only those sustained in motor vehicle accidents but also injuries resulting from workplace accidents not covered by Workers' Compensation and slip and fall accidents in parking lots, public transportation, or grocery stores. While medical malpractice claims theoretically fall under this category, I will deal with them independently.

No matter how minor the injury, the person's body has sustained injuries which doctors refer to as an "insult." This is appropriate because victims feel they have suffered an indignity which has altered their enjoyment of life and negatively influenced the lives of their family and loved ones, their ability to work, and their self-esteem. It doesn't seem to matter whether the victim's future is gravely affected or the injury temporarily affects normal activities such as their ability to golf, dance, skate, or ski.

All disputes concerning responsibility for the accident and the appropriate amount of compensation should be approached with a great degree of sensitivity. That is essential because the victims are often angry and frustrated due to the pain and suffering, the impact of the injury on their ability to work and enjoy life, and concerns about their future. They may also be angry because the claim isn't being settled, and they feel badly treated by the insurer or the insurer's lawyer.

In a typical personal injury lawsuit, the person who actually inflicted the damage is *rarely present* at the mediation. The inflictor is represented by an insurance company adjuster and lawyer who have stepped into the wrongdoer's shoes. The fact that the person who caused the injury is often not present removes the opportunity provided by mediation for the parties to unburden their feelings in a safe way and achieve some closure and healing in the process. If the adjuster understands this and is prepared to take on the role of surrogate wrongdoer, much will be gained. In fact, if the adjuster is sensitive to the dual role, it is much better because if the injuring party were present, other problems might arise. For example, a nonchalant, unrepentant wrongdoer would not help the negotiation climate.

As surrogate for the responsible party, the insurance adjuster should think about the victim's emotional state and prepare to deal with it empathically.

> **TIP** In mediation, where everything is said in confidence under a binding confidentiality agreement, it might be appropriate to apologize on behalf of the wrongdoer, whether or not liability is admitted. While some argue that this will only put wind in the plaintiff's sails, an apology may quench the plaintiff's anger and assist the victim to focus on resolving the matter. Additionally, care should be taken to discuss concepts of shared responsibility in a way that is least offensive to the victim.
>
> The claimant should equally be aware that the adjuster is human and attempting to do her job to the best of her ability. If the fact that the claim isn't settled or any other matters are distressing you, be prepared to tell your story at the mediation in a way that avoids personal attacks on the adjuster.
>
> A properly prepared claimant who speaks for himself about the injury, how it occurred, and its impact on his life, is a much more potent force in negotiation than a silent, intimidated, and passive one. Have no doubt that one of the factors that will weigh heavily in favour of resolving the matter in your favour will be the perception of the impact you would make as a witness at a trial.

Attitudes Towards Mediation

Another unique feature of personal injury cases is the widespread use of surveillance by insurers. A common objection to mediation in cases where the surveillance evidence is compelling goes like this: "If we go to mediation and disclose our evidence, the claimants will adjust their evidence and we'll have lost our opportunity to impugn their credibility." We need to have discoveries so that we can nail down their evidence under oath before we can consider mediation. That way we will be able to get the admissions we need on the record before they change their story.

Here are a couple of observations:

- If the evidence is indeed strong, and is used discreetly like a scalpel rather than a bludgeon in the context of mediation, it should have a considerable moderating effect on the claimant's expectations.

- Since over 95% of cases settle before trial, including those with strong surveillance evidence, early settlement, without the substantial costs of discoveries and a pretrial, is in the best interests of the insurer and insured. In any negotiation the adverse effects of subjecting the claimant to perhaps a gruelling cross-examination and the costs to both parties has to be weighed against the probable negative effect on subsequent negotiations. In litigation there is a direct, and often disproportionate, reaction to every action.

- No matter how evidence is tailored, strong surveillance evidence does not lose its effect. Weak evidence can't be made stronger by springing it suddenly. That only infuriates the victim. Insurers, claimants, and their counsel should reconsider any tendency to approach mediation from a positional as opposed to an interest-based point of view.

• Discoveries cost money—big money. Surely a cost-benefit analysis, if fairly done, will reveal in many cases the benefit of mediating before discovery. Remember that if the mediation does not result in agreement, discoveries may still proceed and very little will have been lost.

Failure to obtain updated medical information, refusing to share it, or wanting to wait until after discovery to obtain independent medical reports in the hope of gaining a tactical advantage, will put the mediation at risk. This kind of approach suggests a positional and strategic approach to the dispute and limits the potential for successful negotiation. A problem-solving, interest-based approach will prove much more successful where information bearing on decisions relating to the case is shared.

Here is an observation for the adjuster:

• Your company is interested in profits, the efficient closure of cases, customer service, and maintaining its reputation for fair dealing. It must, therefore, have an interest in reducing the costs of processing claims and settling them early through mediation.

To the claimant, adjuster, and their lawyers, here are some observations on preparing for mediation:

• You should be able to analyse the settlement value of the case realistically estimating:

 – your costs and theirs for the preparation for discovery and the trial;

 – the costs of medical and other experts;

 – the likelihood of winning or losing on liability; and

 – the likely range of damages.

• If you are secure in your analysis, you shouldn't need a judge or ex-judge to tell you what you already know.

TIP: TO ADJUSTER

Walk in the claimant's shoes and understand that they:
• aren't only interested in the money;
• have been hurt and have suffered a loss;
• have some considerable resentment because the claim hasn't been resolved and *you* are likely being held responsible (whether or not you should be);
• probably fear and loathe the prospect of going to a trial; and
• would rather have the money now than in two to four years.

TIP: TO THE INSURER

- If your company is serious about resolving cases early and efficiently through mediation, you will ensure the adjuster knows this and reward her results accordingly.
- You will communicate your objectives to your lawyers.

TIP: TO THE LAWYER

- You will have to take to heart the interest of your client in early resolution when preparing for and conducting yourself during mediations.
- You should carefully prepare a conservative opinion on the strengths and weaknesses of the case and consider the interests of your opponents as well as your client's. Be prepared to engage in a negotiation based on these interests. Remember, mediation requires a bona fide intention to negotiate a fair outcome for both parties. It is not a time for unrealistic expectations, nor should it be used as a device for gaining an advantage in the litigation.
- Prior to the mediation, obtain and share all critically important information with your opponent. Demand no less from your counterpart.

Case Study

A husband and wife were severely injured and were both confined to wheelchairs as a result of a multicar collision in 1988. The scene of the accident was chaotic, with cars everywhere. The police reports and witness statements were contradictory, confusing, and frankly of little assistance apart from noting the approximate place where the vehicle came to rest. Lengthy discoveries had been conducted; however, confusion about the cause of the accident remained.

The claimants' medical condition remained unaltered for three years before the case was mediated in 1995, seven years after the accident. While valiant efforts were directed at determining the precise chain of events and responsibility for the accident, the long-suffering claimants had been languishing on the back burner. At no time during the seven-year period had any leadership been taken because the legal system encourages everyone to minimize their exposure, at the expense of others. Everyone was blaming the other guy in the hope of escaping responsibility and spending a lot of money in the process.

At the mediation everyone came together for the first time in seven years. Thirteen insurance companies and their lawyers saw the unfortunate claimants for the first time as a group. The enormity of the oversight in settling the claim was quickly apparent and their claim was settled. The question of apportionment between the various players was short work based on rough calculations and divided between them when they realized that the total amount paid to the claimants divided by thirteen paled in comparison to the costs of a trial, including the expense of numerous experts' reports.

They also knew that the long-suffering claimants would undoubtedly succeed and that someone would have to pay. Furthermore, the courts are becoming increasingly intolerant of delays bordering on the outrageous and they are penalizing such behaviour by awarding costs or punitive damages. The case was resolved because each defendant no longer viewed the matter in isolation as solely their problem. While working together, pooling the information and expertise at hand, a very good picture emerged as to the likely outcome of a trial on the question of apportionment of liability.

I was struck by the professionalism and preparation of all concerned in resolving the entire matter in less than five hours. They simply had not had the opportunity or collective will to meet earlier due to the number of parties and the adversarial system.

DISABILITY CLAIMS

A recent study conducted by one insurance company cited an experiment involving eleven disability claims, ten of which were settled through mediation and one by arbitration. Six were mediated prior to discovery. The most significant fact from the insurers' perspective is that *25% of the total reserves set aside to cover the potential exposure were used to settle the claims, pay the fees of the lawyer and mediator.* In other words, the insurance company had allocated three times the actual cost of resolving these claims as a reasonable estimate of the cost to settle if they continued in the litigation stream. This is not surprising when you consider the cost of independent medical reports and witness fees for doctors and forensic accountants, coupled with the costs of discovery and trial.

Other advantages include satisfied policyholders and avoiding bad legal precedents. A bad precedent may be relied upon by many others in similar circumstances and may be a significant problem for life and health insurers in terms of increased payments to claimants and the inevitable raising of premiums that follows.

Mediation is well suited to disability claims for several reasons:

• There are usually highly emotional components to these cases.

- They are conducted in private and subject to a confidentiality agreement.

- Adverse precedents may be avoided in difficult cases.

- The issues are usually confined to one or two questions involving whether the claimant is entitled to payment, the period of entitlement, medical issues, and the amount of compensation.

- The amounts involved usually pale in comparison to the costs of litigation.

Case Study

A senior executive was disabled by chronic depression following a series of personal catastrophes. The claim was paid by the disability insurer for two years when surveillance evidence suggested that the claimant was resuming business activities part-time. That meant the insurers could stop payments. They did, abruptly and with little explanation. In its Statement of Defence, the insurance company accused the executive of malingering and dishonesty. These accusations produced considerable anger and a determination on his part to obtain public vindication of his good name and reputation through the courts. Suddenly the case was about a lot more than money.

During the mediation the insurer had the opportunity to assess the credibility of the executive. His activities were explained to their satisfaction, when they learned that the activity mistaken for business was philanthropic and related to family investments. The executive had not returned to his previous occupation or started a new business.

A written apology was sincerely offered and accepted together with all the missed payments. An amount was agreed upon to buy out or redeem the policy so that neither party would have any continuing obligations to the other, a not uncommon outcome of the bitterness engendered by litigation. Both parties were pleased to be out of a lawsuit that might have gone either way.

DIVORCE AND FAMILY MEDIATION

There is a long tradition of mediating family disputes in Canada, although they have been exempted in Ontario from mandatory mediation. The precise reasoning for this exemption is not known. If certain family cases are inappropriate candidates for mediation, an opting-out provision might have been included or it may simply have been a question of timing for that particular sector and that in the fullness of time court-connected mediation will become routine in family disputes.

Family disputes ought to be mediated whenever possible. Even a simple uncontested divorce case of a childless couple, where the only issue is the division of assets, can greatly benefit from mediation. Notwithstanding the apparent simplicity, divorce is about ending a long-standing, intimate relationship. Even in a simple case, the emotional element will be substantial and will vary tremendously from case to case. In the absence of agreement, complex laws govern the distribution of these assets. The use of litigation to resolve these cases has an abysmal record of failure. The system encourages extreme positions and exacerbates already raw emotions.

Reputable family mediators are able to help divorcing couples with both the complex legal and legislative framework and the emotional side of a divorce with sensitivity and neutrality. Appropriate mediators should have no bias or preconceived ideas. It would not be at all inappropriate to inquire about the proposed mediator's marital and family history. While it is not customary for the lawyers to participate in all family sessions, their attendance will be useful for specific issues, such as the division of the assets and putting together the separation agreement.

When children are involved and issues of child or spousal support, custody, and access are added to the mix, the emotional and financial ante goes up considerably. The mediator's main task is to assist the parents to negotiate their continued involvement with each other and their children. The objective is to foster a good working relationship between the parents in the interest of the well-being of the children. The potential for the litigation process to work its destructive magic in cases involving children increases exponentially.

The choice of mediator is critical. Consideration should be given to consulting with your doctor, pastor, and lawyer. If mediation has not been suggested by your lawyer, you will want to ensure she not only supports the process but is capable of assisting you throughout or has a very sound reason for opposing mediation.

Mediation is not therapy. Mediation is not about reconciliation, although that may be one of the results and should not be precluded by the parties or the mediator as a possibility, however remote. On the other hand, parties whose main objective is reconciliation should seek out the services of a family therapist or counsellor.

The primary goal of family mediation is to resolve the dispute through agreement between the parties, an agreement which they create with the help and support of the mediator. If the parties need to learn to communicate or acquire other skills in order to achieve a durable agreement, a qualified family mediator will provide the necessary coaching before the parties are allowed to meet together. This may involve several sessions with the parties separately to ensure that face-to-face meetings, when they occur, will be positive and productive. The important thing is to choose the appropriate mediator based on the needs of the situation and the individuals. In some cases where mental or physical abuse is involved, a mediator with a medical background in concert with the parties' lawyers would be appropriate. The material in Chapter 4 will assist you to select an experienced mediator.

In some cases, mediation may be inappropriate or may have to be structured for the safety of the participants. In some cases the parties may not be able to meet face to face until a climate of respect and commitment to problem solving is achieved. An experienced mediator will design an appropriate process after the initial separate interviews are completed.

Case Study

A middle-aged husband and wife separated due to irreconcilable differences after five years of marriage. The husband, a successful professional at the time of separation, suffered career and financial reversals due to corporate restructuring. The wife, whose career was placed on hold to raise a young daughter, rejoined the workforce shortly after the separation and enjoyed considerable success, eventually surpassing the husband's income.

A separation agreement which had been drawn up shortly after separation, based child-support payments on the husband's high income at the date of separation but contained a provision allowing for reduction in support payments if there was a material change in either the husband's or wife's circumstances.

The agreement provided for mediation in the event of a dispute. During the husband's period of unemployment and after he secured a job at 60% of his former income, requests for a reduction in support payments had gone unheeded as had a request to have the matter resolved through mediation. Apparently the wife was being advised by her lawyer to resist mediation despite the provision in the agreement. The wife eventually switched lawyers. The new lawyer recommended that the mediation proceed, as there was nothing to lose and everything to be gained if the matter could be resolved without a trial.

Prior to the mediation, the mediator suggested that the first session should be conducted with the parties separated as they were unable to communicate directly. Although the mediation was ostensibly about changing the financial support paid by the husband, it quickly became apparent that a host of issues required attention, including the wife's need for financial stability, the parents' relationship with their daughter, the feelings of alienation and lack of involvement in the child's life experienced by the father, his perception that the wife was using every opportunity to reduce the child's esteem for him, and the wife's failure to proceed to obtain the divorce as required by the separation agreement.

During the mediation the parties were able to express their negative feelings towards each other safely and achieve a measure of closure with respect to the failed marriage. More importantly, they were able to agree that the welfare and happiness of the child was a shared and paramount interest. A number of creative suggestions emerged which dealt with the father's concerns and need for more involvement with his daughter including close cooperation relating to school and after-school activities, more frequent and flexible access by telephone and in person, and a provision whereby the wife undertook to promote whenever possible a positive relationship between the father and child. Information was shared relating to their income and expenses, and an objective standard was agreed to which would determine ongoing support based on an annual review and revision.

Perhaps the largest gain in the process was that by the fourth session, the parties were calmly discussing the issues face to face and proposing options to resolve the problems. They had learned a lot about each other's points of view and were now able to communicate without the anger and hostility normally engendered by the litigation process. The cost of the four sessions and the legal advice required to settle their agreement was under five thousand dollars, a small fraction of the cost of litigation. They also agreed to mediate any future disputes.

EMPLOYMENT DISPUTES

Mediation lends itself particularly well to employment disputes because there are usually only two parties involved: the employee and the employer. The issues are generally straightforward and limited in number. Either the dismissal was wrongful or it was not. Did the employer have "just cause" to end the relationship? If not, what is appropriate notice or compensation and did the employee take reasonable steps to find suitable alternate employment? Calculation of the appropriate amount of compensation is all that remains. If there is a plausible argument that the employment was unjustly terminated, the employee must decide whether the matter ought to be taken to court.

If there are a number of good reasons for resolving the matter out of court, then mediation is ideally suited to deal with the matter. The amount of money involved in these cases is usually less than one year's salary. Contrast that with the cost of litigation which, even in simple cases will exceed fifteen or twenty thousand dollars per party.

Reasons why the employer might opt for mediation include the time and expense of litigation, but also the cost of corporate resources such as employees taking time off work to give evidence at trial. The negative message litigating sends back to the troops and the potentially harmful publicity if the trial is lost, deserve careful attention by employers. Employers have an interest in avoiding a reputation for hard-nosed bargaining and strategic use of the justice system to reduce severance costs.

Emotions

Like divorce and family mediation, employment disputes are emotionally charged. People identify closely with their jobs, form close ties with co-workers, and take pride in their accomplishments. When the employment relationship ends, even if the reasons are valid, such as in downsizing, reorganization, or rationalization, the loss has a huge impact on an individual's self-esteem. Add to the mix the employee's perception that the termination wasn't well or sensitively handled and the difficulties frequently encountered in finding replacement employment, and you have fertile ground for anger and resentment. If, after six months, the individual is still unemployed, those feelings are exacerbated by the humiliation of having to subsist on employment insurance.

From both the employee's and employer's perspective, mediation is hugely beneficial if only because 98% of the time it can be done without requiring discovery. It bears repeating that in these cases costs of litigation are a significant feature to both employer and employee. Compensation recoverable in wrongful dismissal litigation is usually measured, as a rough rule of thumb, by awarding a month of compensation for every year of service. Early resolution without both sides consuming scarce resources in the discovery process increases the net amount available to the employee.

Mediation is of significant benefit to employees because it allows them to discuss openly how they felt about their dismissal. The opportunity to do this in a safe environment is an important component in bringing closure to that chapter in their life. This opportunity is unavailable in a courtroom. Early closure allows the employee to focus on getting on with the job search, free of the distractions associated with a pending lawsuit.

From the employer's perspective, they may feel personally sympathetic to the individual but equally strongly that the best interests of the company are paramount, particularly if performance issues were involved, such as continued low productivity and costly errors despite numerous warnings and coaching attempts. These sentiments may be expressed less harshly in the mediation setting than in the stark, sometimes extreme, language of court documents.

Who represents the company at the mediation is critical. In smaller companies, the president or another senior officer will often attend with his lawyer. In larger companies, the vice-president of human relations or an equivalent should attend.

> **TIP**   Do not send someone who had a problematic relationship with the employee. Do not bring "witnesses" to relate first-hand stories of non-performance or malfeasance. While such items may be features of the company's attitude towards the individual and may have informed its decision to terminate, the company representative at mediation should be objective and appear reasonable to the employee if progress is to be made. Remember, the employee is the ultimate decision maker when it comes to settling. Sending a company representative who is appropriately senior and who is able to empathize, take responsibility, and make decisions will pay dividends. If the strong emotional element is not dealt with sensitively, all too often the employee simply will not be in a position to make rational choices, even if the company's offer to resolve is generous.

Preparation

Preparation on both sides is critical. The employee must work through as best he can all the emotions surrounding the termination. Spend some time reading the anger section in Chapter 5 before the mediation.

The employee should prepare a binder with a copy of the employment contract, job description and compensation package, details of job-search activities and any costs involved, and their income during the period. Particulars should be included of any employment insurance payments received. Performance appraisals are also relevant.

The employer should have complete details of the employee's terms of employment, compensation and benefits, employment record, and job description. Some time might be spent usefully thinking about the employee's current circumstances and whether relocation or other assistance might be of benefit to the employee. Remember, often it isn't just about money. It may be about uncertainty, fear, future prospects, and bitterness.

The Agreement to Resolve

Agreements to resolve wrongful dismissal cases often contain creative elements which courts are unable to award. Such agreements have included:

- outplacement assistance;
- retraining assistance;
- assistance with introductions and networking;
- reference letters and a designated person who fields reference call using a agreed-upon scripted response;
- apologies;

- structured settlements to maximize taxation effectiveness through payments into RRSPs;
- even reinstatement of the employee in her old job or a similar position with a related company.

A court is not able to order any of these things. During the mediation some lawyers tend to concentrate on items that are within the jurisdiction of the court, namely, compensation and costs. Often the need for these other elements only emerges during the mediation process.

Case Study

A man was fired by the retailing company he had worked for since leaving high school thirty-six years before. He had advanced to department manager and had only four years to retirement.

At the mediation it emerged that the employee had been asked to train his replacement for two months prior to the termination on the pretext that he was being trained for another department. The circumstances surrounding the termination were less than ideal. His immediate superior called him in on a Friday morning to tell him he was fired. The employee asked why but apparently was told nothing. The store manager and manager of human relations kept themselves out of the process and refused to see or even meet with him. No references were offered and the bare minimum severance was tendered.

The employee immediately found another job at slightly less pay but sued anyway. During the mediation it was obvious that the driving force behind the lawsuit was anger at his treatment. Throughout the mediation the employee was highly controlled. However, the financial demands being made were so unrealistic that it was clear the employee was not interested in simply settling the case. He wanted revenge.

The company was represented by the manager of human relations who had previously refused to meet with the employee. At one point in joint session, the employee was overcome by emotion and burst into a tirade of accusations about the way he had been treated after such long service. Having achieved a certain amount of satisfaction and catharsis, the employee readily agreed to moderate his compensation demands in exchange for a letter of reference. Unfortunately, the manager of human resources was so shaken and unprepared for the emotional outpouring that she was unable to regroup and retired from the mediation hastily with lawyer in tow. The matter was settled on mutually agreeable terms shortly thereafter.

I cite this case of "failed" mediation to illustrate the importance of having the appropriate representative present as well as the inestimable value of careful preparation, including being prepared to handle the presence of strong emotions.

FAMILY BUSINESS DISPUTES

Thousands of businesses in Canada are family owned, from giants like McCain Foods, Canadian Tire, and WIC International, to mom-and-pop corner stores. Litigation in family business disputes is simply not an option if the sad stories that appear in the newspapers from time to time are to be avoided. The very essence of a family business is the family relationship. Keeping conflict from adversely affecting the value of the business and the family relationship is the goal of every family business manager. These businesses are not run solely for profit. Decisions are constrained by emotional ties. Family conflict has the potential to be much more destructive and volatile than simple office politics, and they can affect future generations.

Disputes may erupt between individual members or branches of the family about succession, money, management styles, and corporate initiatives such as sale of assets or expansion. Founders or owners are often reluctant to hand over the reins to the next generation. Mediation is ideally suited to these disputes. It is private, and avoids the embarrassment of displaying the family's dirty laundry in public. Also it can be tailored to suit the dispute.

Employing an experienced mediator, perceived by all the family as neutral, will be of tremendous assistance to founders and family business managers in avoiding the worst aspects of these conflicts. While ignoring the problems may seem like an attractive alternative, the result of deferring family disputes is usually debilitating and ultimately destructive of the family business which, if healthy, could provide financial security for many generations.

Family Councils—Preventative Medicine

An ounce of prevention is worth a pound of cure. Putting in place dispute-management processes will pay handsome dividends for the family business. This can be achieved through family councils. A neutral party is retained by the family to convene and facilitate regular periodic family meetings. Attendance is based not on the business hierarchy but membership in the family. The initial meetings work towards producing a charter which will govern the family council and provide family advice and input, but not direction, to the managers of the business. Typically, these charters contain detailed dispute resolution provisions which family members agree to observe in the event of a conflict. These charters acknowledge the family relationship by including all members. Unlike typical business managements, they are democratic and allow every family member to give voice to their feelings and concerns in an environment that is safe. While family councils are only advisory, they perform an invaluable function by providing guidance to the business managers and an outlet and forum for the resolution of inevitable disagreements of family life.

CONSTRUCTION CASES

Resolving construction disputes quickly and efficiently has been a concern within the industry and government for decades. The problems stem from the way construction projects are structured. Usually the owner hires architects or engineers to design a building or project. There will be a contract between them for this work. Then, armed with details of the project from the architect, the owner puts the construction of the project out to tender. Several general contractors may bid on the job, one is selected and a contract is signed, usually a standard form agreement with appropriate amendments. The general contractor will then turn around and contract with numerous subcontractors (excavation, concrete, steel, mechanical, and electrical, to name a few). They, in turn, contract with suppliers of materials. There are no contractual obligations between the owner and subcontractors or materials suppliers, nor between the architect and subcontractor or material suppliers.

Over the years this complex web of interrelationships and the protracted litigation arising from construction disputes has perplexed everyone associated with the industry, including those who finance and insure the completion of projects. The best solution devised has been the "construction lien" which, essentially, by legislation, imposes a relationship on all the players in the construction pyramid, from the owner at the apex to the suppliers at its base. Despite efforts in the legislation to make the lien process speedy, inexpensive, and efficient, experience has been woeful on all counts.

Given the complex interrelationship of the parties and extreme potential for conflict, mediation is appropriate in almost all construction cases. These include insurance claims or performance bonds, claims for extras and breaches of contract by owners and contractors, or professional negligence by consultants. Mediation is recognized as the preferred first line of dispute resolution in the Canadian Construction Document Committee (CCDC) standard form general contract. While distinctive in many ways, construction disputes lend themselves to mediation, provided care is taken to recognize the differences inherent in these types of disputes.

Some of the distinctions which ought to be appreciated are:

- Many disputes arise as the construction project progresses. If they are not dealt with very early, they tend to spawn additional conflict, with the result that the climate on the job may become poisoned. The beauty of mediation in this context is that it can be convened quickly, thus preserving the continuing relationship of the parties during the critical construction period.

- Construction disputes are often technical in nature and relate to interpretations of drawings or specifications and other tender documents. Conflicts may arise over construction methods and proper costing of changes to the contracts or claims for delay, directions (or lack of them) by consultants, architects, and engineers.

The choice of mediator in these cases is all-important. That person should possess not only mediation skills but the ability to understand the technical construction issues. In the many construction cases where experts are required, the mediator, may play a role in assisting the parties to agree on a neutral expert to advise the parties and the mediator thus preventing a "battle of the experts" which can widen, rather than narrow, the rift.

Construction Liens

- The *Construction Lien Act* creates a legislative framework to settle disputes in construction and to provide security to parties who do not have a direct contractual relationship with the owner. The courts oversee the application of this legislation which requires the parties to attend at court for pretrial meetings and settlement conferences. Experience has indicated that the courts are far less effective than mediation which is flexible and speedy.

- There are often multiple parties involved in construction cases. This may be particularly so in cases of construction lien claims or claims for extras or delay. The challenge in these cases is designing a process that ensures that the right people are at the table at the appropriate time in what may be a two- or three-session mediation.

Partnering

Because of the ongoing nature of the relationship during the construction, especially of large projects and because multiple parties are involved, a dispute prevention and resolution process called "partnering" was developed by the U.S. Corps of Engineers in response to the incidence of claims and burgeoning costs of litigation.

This concept recognizes that construction is a team effort and encourages team building prior to the commencement of a project. Partnering presupposes a substantial commitment from the highest level of each organization involved. Team-building sessions are held before construction begins. Facilitated by a neutral, the goal is to personalize the project from the top down by creating one-on-one relationships between the various levels of interaction. The theory for this is that it is harder to fight with someone you know and trust.

The team-building exercise is also designed to produce a charter which commits each signatory to bringing the job in on time and on (or under) budget. The charter contains a detailed dispute resolution framework with specific time frames required to work the matter up the chain of command until it is resolved. If the parties fail to negotiate an agreement between themselves, a "project mediator," usually named in the charter, is called in to convene a mediation.

While in its infancy in Canada, experience both here and in the United States is very encouraging. Partnering has been used successfully by the Ontario Ministry of Transportation in a number of large road-construction projects. Time will undoubtedly evolve a "made-in-Canada" system of partnering tailored to the way the Canadian construction industry operates, which will ensure even greater utilization of this promising process.

Case Study

During construction of a church, the owner and the general contractor were involved in an acrimonious dispute involving information supplied by the architect on site conditions, excavation, and grading. The contractor claimed the information was wrong and that it cost several hundred thousand dollars to correct the mistake. The church had to be completed before September to meet commitments to its congregation for the provision of a day care and religious schooling. The lease of their temporary facility was not renewable and the church faced the prospect of having to vacate in August.

The file was three inches thick with the letters between the contractor and architect becoming more and more heated by the day. Accusations and cross-accusations about misleading instructions relating to other costs were exchanged regularly and there were suggestions by the contractor that the architect had been negligent. Meanwhile, the project schedule fell further and further behind and the September completion date started looking like wishful thinking.

To their credit, the lawyers for both parties realized that litigation simply was not practical. The mediation was convened in July. During the first session, the parties worked out a pragmatic and objective method of valuing the extra work, together with an appropriate division of the costs. Further information was required to resolve the grading and excavation claim. This information was obtained. The architect's insurer became involved and the parties reconvened within a week. In addition, a schedule for the completion of the work was negotiated with each party agreeing to share half the overtime costs. The project was completed on time, thus averting a major catastrophe for the owner and a protracted and costly lawsuit for both parties.

The tendency in construction is often to approach resolution of the conflict in a win/lose bottom line (positional mode). This is due, in part, to the culture of construction, often described as the last bastion of the self-reliant, rugged individualist. It also has to do with the fact that individuals in the construction industry take great pride in their work. They believe their reputation is at stake in many of these disputes. In order to assist in changing the culture, construction lawyers will have to provide leadership and become better versed in interest-based negotiation and mediation. Construction lawyers are not the cause of the problem but to some extent are prisoners of the lien legislation and industry attitudes. The construction industry as a whole must become better acquainted with the benefits of an interest-based problem-solving approach to resolving their disputes and insist that mediation be attempted before resorting to litigation.

Care should be taken to select a mediator with industry experience. The mediator should also have a legal background given the legal and legislative framework that will inform much of the discussion in most disputes.

ESTATE DISPUTES

Estate Planning—Preventing Disputes

Our parents and their parents had it fairly easy when it came to planning how their estate would be divided. Not only were their assets relatively modest, so were the taxation and inheritance laws. Things have changed drastically, and not for the better:

• Unprecedented economic prosperity has led to significant growth of middle-class wealth. The "boomers" are on the threshold of inheriting trillions of dollars worth of property and assets from their hard-working and frugal parents and grandparents.

• Taxation of estates, trusts, and the fees payable on death have become a costly and complex minefield for the unwary.

• Second and third marriages are more the rule than the exception. Treating children from the later marriages equitably and legally may be a challenge for those drafting wills.

• The number of new small businesses, particularly family ones, is growing exponentially as the fallout from restructuring and downsizing drives those affected to start-up their own.

• The trend towards using self-help kits to prepare wills or looking for a bargain-basement deal from paralegals or lawyers who only dabble in will preparation will result in an increased number of estate disputes as short-term savings at the expense of quality takes its toll.

There is a great deal of potential for conflict in matters involving entitlement to inheritances, business succession, minimization of taxes and fees, and improper powers of attorney. Taking the time to create a workable estate plan will prevent or at least minimize conflict that may otherwise be inevitable if these issues are left unattended.

An extremely useful estate-planning tool is to provide in your will that in the event of a dispute arising among the beneficiaries, if anyone contests the will, a mediator will be appointed (by the court if the parties cannot agree) to assist in resolving the dispute before litigation is started.

Estate Disputes

Conflict occurs when individuals feel they have not been treated fairly. Issues that give rise to disputes will include the testator's mental capacity, claims arising under the *Family Law Act* or the *Dependent's Relief Act*, undue influence exercised over the testator, and whether the will was properly signed. The fact that families are involved makes these disputes particularly amenable to mediation because the family relationship is in jeopardy. Family fights left unattended take years or even generations to repair.

Until recently there was no alternative to litigation if negotiations between the parties, the executors, and their lawyers failed. Mediation is ideally suited to resolving estate disputes for many reasons. Consider the following:

- The importance of achieving family harmony and preserving family relationships is a major consideration. The fact that most estate disputes are emotionally highly charged makes them ideally suited to mediation.
- The family's privacy is protected. Avoiding the glare of publicity or notoriety will have strong appeal in most cases. Moral considerations may be more directly and delicately addressed through negotiation.
- The need to avoid unnecessary "shrinkage" of the estate is vital. Formal legal proceedings are costly and the legal costs of most proceedings are usually paid out of the estate. Reduced costs are a direct benefit to all the beneficiaries.
- Agreements to resolve disputes achieved through negotiation may be far more flexible and creative. Equitable results are more readily achieved than may be possible in court.

Given what we know about the amount of time consumed by litigation, the cost of motions for directions, discoveries, pretrial and trials, as well as the almost certain rise of acrimony as the process unfolds, attempting mediation before resorting to litigation only makes good sense.

In weighing these factors before making any decisions on the most appropriate route to follow, those involved might consider the choice the testator would have made between mediation or litigation, had he known his last wishes would result in a nasty lawsuit involving loved ones.

The leadership required to establish mediation as a legitimate and highly desirable means of settling estate disputes must be provided by those with the most to gain—you, the affected party! If your advisors are unsure of the benefits of early, inexpensive negotiated settlements that accommodate all affected parties, you may wish to obtain a second opinion.

Case Study

A father of three daughters died leaving his estate to the eldest, naming her his executrix, and cutting out his wife of forty-five years and the other two daughters. The testator had been separated from his wife for three years although there was no separation agreement. The family was completely dysfunctional; the sisters and mother had not spoken in years. The estate, valued at between $300,000 and $400,000, consisted of a house and contents and several building lots in rural northern Ontario.

The two daughters who received nothing were challenging the will for a number of reasons. The wife had commenced a separate action for unpaid support payments and a large claim under the *Dependent's Relief Act* (legislation designed to protect dependents not adequately provided for in the will).

During a separate mediation of the sisters' claim, the favoured daughter was able to demonstrate to her sisters the amount of money, time, and work she and her husband had spent during the past ten years maintaining the father and his house. With help from their lawyers and an appraisal, they agreed on an appropriate division of the assets which recognized the eldest daughter's claim but otherwise treated them equally. This agreement was conditional on the resolution of their mother's dispute. The mother was contacted through her lawyer and happily agreed to attend a second mediation session.

Much of the discussion at this session centred on family issues and old resentments. It was clear that without discussing these long-unattended wounds the matter would not have been resolved. More importantly, it was clear to the mother and her children that a golden opportunity had been presented to begin the hard work of restoring their relationship.

This case is cited for two reasons. The total cost for both sessions of the mediation was under $2,500 for each participant. Had both cases been litigated through discoveries and trial, the value of the estate would have been depleted by as much as $100,000. Far more important than the money is the saving of human costs. The dispute served to bring the parties together in a non-confrontational way, instead of driving a wedge further between them, and assisted them to begin to overcome their troubled past.

BANKRUPTCY AND INSOLVENCY

Bankruptcy and insolvency matters consume enormous quantities of social capital and take a large emotional and financial toll on society. It is not by accident that the term "Vulture Fund" was coined to define those who pick over the carcass of bankrupt companies. The legislation governing bankruptcy and insolvency is every bit as complex as the construction statutes, and the battles between various classes of creditors every bit as fractious. Some of the reasons for mediating disputes between debtors and creditors follow.

Timeliness

Time is everyone's enemy in insolvency matters as assets waste and accounting and legal costs mount. Rather than picking over the bones of a dead carcass, creditors and debtors may, with the help of the mediator, actually breathe new life into a troubled business. The sooner the parties come to grips with the problems, the better.

Complexity

Bankruptcy cases frequently involve limited assets and numerous parties, such as suppliers, multiple classes of creditors (secured, unsecured), and often the Crown. The relatively new bankruptcy laws in Canada and lack of judicial interpretation will cause much uncertainty until the law is well settled. This state of flux provides a good reason for parties to attempt to negotiate their own result. In mediation, negotiations are conducted under the aegis of a confidentiality agreement, not through the media which usually adds to the difficulties in achieving resolution.

Flexibility

Mediation puts control into the hands of the parties who are free to move quickly. Not all parties need attend all the meetings. The process may be fine-tuned to respond to the facts far better than a court-supervised process. While court approval may be required, court supervision of negotiations is not.

Problem Solving and Consensus Building

Mediation preserves rather than impairs relationships, which is the usual result of litigation. This is especially relevant considering the current legislative emphasis on salvaging jobs and businesses through the use of creative proposals and reorganizations, rather than simply liquidating the assets and selling them off at "fire sale prices." Interest-based negotiation which emphasizes that all parties be at the table and carefully examine their alternatives, is ideally suited to bankruptcy and insolvency cases.

Choice of Mediator

While it is for the court, not the mediator, to approve any plans of reorganization or proposals put forward under bankruptcy or insolvency legislation, the mediator in these cases should possess both strong mediation skills and a good working knowledge of bankruptcy and insolvency issues and the applicable legislation.

Process

While timely resolution is possible, all parties to a bankruptcy or insolvency mediation should be patient. Representatives of various classes of creditors must have time to consult their constituents. Time should be allotted to digest and obtain information relevant to intelligent decision making. Separate meetings between the mediator and overly aggressive groups may be necessary in order to succeed in producing consensus. In these cases, several sessions over a number of weeks may be required. Even so, this is nothing compared to the way these cases could drag on for months and years in the courts.

Emotion

The atmosphere surrounding a bankruptcy may be highly emotional. Creditors usually feel betrayed or deceived. Management of the bankrupt company and individuals forced to declare bankruptcy will feel ashamed and humiliated. The mediation process, if skilfully conducted, permits parties to safely vent their feelings and better understand the factors which led to the failure. The process also puts pressure on all parties to put their feelings behind them and to focus on making a decision consistent with improving their future prospects.

Court Supervision Not Dismissed

Because the issues surrounding bankruptcy and insolvency affect so many people's fundamental interests, it is important that these matters not be resolved behind closed doors. I am not suggesting this. The court's jurisdiction isn't dismissed by mediation. The court is, however, used sparingly to fine-tune the mediated agreement, rather than as a nursemaid shepherding the matter step by expensive, time-consuming step through the process, a task more efficiently performed by the mediator. If impasse arises during the course of the mediation, the court is there for direction.

Case Study

A sporting goods retailer, Smith Sports Stores, was approached by an American conglomerate, Big Box Sport. Smith Stores was interested in merging with Big Box who dangled a number of attractive incentives including an offer to immediately assist Smith in financing its sales at a much higher level. Coincidentally, Smith was negotiating with the All Canadian Junior League to supply their entire equipment and uniform needs for a three-year period, a contract valued at over $500,000.

Smith, relying on Big's assurances, hastily placed an order worth $350,000 with the baseball equipment company, EQUIPCO, to manufacture the gloves, balls, bats, and uniforms for the first two years. EQUIPCO, having doubts about Smith's financial strength, requested a joint purchase order from both the Junior League and Smith Stores. The Junior Leaguers refused and threatened to place their order elsewhere.

Smith persuaded EQUIPCO to accept a post-dated cheque which EQUIPCO agreed to hold until advised by Smith Stores that they had the money from the Junior League to cover it. EQUIPCO only accepted the post-dated cheque on the strength of Big Box's imminent merger with Smith. The equipment and uniforms were shipped to the Junior Leaguers during the last week of February. The same week Big Box pulled out of the deal with Smith.

Without the support of Big Box, Smith Stores was unable to pay EQUIPCO who retained lawyers and demanded immediate payment. The Junior Leaguers were advised that to pay EQUIPCO would be to give one of Smith's many creditors a preference which would expose the Junior League to legal liability.

Al and Pete Smith, the principals of Smith Stores, held security over the assets of the stores for money they had lent to Smith Stores over the years. They took steps to realize on their security by demanding that the Junior League pay them the $350,000.

Typical of bankruptcy and insolvency matters, there was a fierce competition for the $350,000. EQUIPCO harboured ill feelings towards the Smith brothers believing that the whole Junior League deal was a scam by the Smiths to "bulk up" the assets of Smith Stores and pay off their loans before the company went bankrupt.

At the time of the mediation, the following legal proceedings had occurred:

- The Smith brothers had appointed a "Receiver and Manager" under their security agreement to obtain the funds from the Junior League to pay off their loan.

- EQUIPCO had issued a Bankruptcy Petition against Smith Stores and the Smith brothers.

- Smith brothers and Smith Stores counter-claimed on their security agreement for the repayment of their loans.

- The Junior League agreed to pay $350,000 jointly to Smith Stores and EQUIPCO.
- Discoveries had been completed and each party had spent $26,000 in legal and accounting fees.

During the mediation it emerged that Al Smith enjoyed a close relationship with the president of EQUIPCO, Steve Ward, since they were both born in the same small town in Scotland. Steve felt betrayed and humiliated—betrayed because of the friendship, humiliated because he had waived the company policy of obtaining joint purchase orders for large orders.

The Smiths were able to demonstrate their good faith and prove to the satisfaction of EQUIPCO that they were not fattening the assets and that Big Box's pull-out, as well as being untimely, was totally unanticipated. They were also able to agree that continued litigation would further deplete the assets by $75,000 to $100,000. They resolved the matter by dividing the $350,000 equally in recognition that winning or losing was a fifty-fifty proposition. Furthermore, and just as important, Al and Steve had reconciled their differences and would continue to do business with one another.

MULTIPARTY/MULTIISSUE DISPUTES

We are all too familiar with the type of gridlock and political shuffling that results when traditional dispute resolution methods are used to decide on new locations for garbage dumps and dams, or new city infrastructure. The legitimate interests of fishermen, environmentalists, energy-starved businesses, various levels of government, and drought-prone farmers often collide, producing little of value.

Whenever the rights of a number of stakeholders are affected by a proposed development, such a mine, timber cutting, energy or commercial development, mediation can play a valuable role in providing not only a forum for diversely affected groups such as conservationists, business interests, aboriginal peoples, and agencies representing the public interest, but actually provide solutions for achieving and sustaining development.

The single most important characteristic of mediation is its flexibility to accommodate widely opposing views, allowing diehard adversaries to sit side by side productively in a problem-solving mode. Another advantage of mediation is the ability to expand or contract the table as required to accommodate relevant voices. Experienced mediators will design a process which can quickly identify the important issues, strike an agenda, and work towards collaborative solutions while empowering those whose views might otherwise be drowned out.

The most difficult tasks encountered in such mediations is ensuring that balanced and complete information is available to all participants, that power imbalances are addressed, and that the issues are properly defined. When the participants are fully committed to the process and sufficient financial resources are dedicated, remarkable success has been achieved.

Mediator's Knowledge of the Issues

In complex multiparty disputes, the mediator's expertise and knowledge of the technical components in dispute is at a premium. Large construction projects involving many layers of contractual responsibility and natural resource developments involving aboriginal land claims, governments, corporate and environmental concerns, require a balance of substantive knowledge and traditional mediator skills.

During these lengthy mediations, what seems to happen to opposing, often hostile parties by virtue of spending time together in the process of refining and clarifying issues is that these competing groups begin to develop the capacity to view the dispute from the other side's point of view while also achieving a measure of grudging respect, in place of hostility and frustration. This new-found climate helps to build solutions. Achieving this group dynamic is simply not possible through litigation or processes designed to deliver a decision which favours one interest over another.

When all the legitimate interests and concerns are tabled through negotiation, if one group remains steadfastly unyielding, it may be isolated by its inflexibility. The walk-away position—for example, an application for an injunction—may be intact, but it may be isolated. The group's chances of success will probably diminish and the project will enjoy a much better chance of success.

MEDICAL MALPRACTICE

Much of what is discussed under Personal Injury Claims on page 127 is equally true of medical malpractice claims. The claimant has suffered harm and feels strongly that it could have been avoided. I use the term medical malpractice loosely and intend it to apply to claims against any health-care professional, a group including hospitals, dentists, general practitioners, pediatricians, chiropractors, physiotherapists, podiatrists, naturopaths, psychiatrists, psychologists, and even veterinarians. Some of the facts which have to be taken into account when considering mediation of medical claims are:

- Health-care professionals have a significant interest, individually and generally in preserving their professional reputation for providing excellent care. Hospital insurers have a similar interest in defending their staffs.

- The medical professions tend to control their own insurance programmes, as do other professionals, such as lawyers and engineers.

- Claims arising from the level of care received at the hands of a doctor, whether in his office or at the hospital, are self-insured through the Canadian Medical Protective Association (CMPA). (Other health-care providers are either self-insured or are covered for negligence by conventional policies issued by insurance companies.) The current policy approach of the CMPA is to defend all cases and take them to trial where there is a "defensible case." Essentially, a defensible case is defined as one where the doctor's care (supported by an appropriate expert opinion) arguably did not fall below the legally required standard.

- Doctors and other health-care professionals are under pressure from governments to keep their compensation expectations modest while at the same time they must pay high insurance levies to the CMPA to fund the cost of all claims and costs. Hospitals who employ nurses, technicians, and aides are also under increasing pressure to cut costs.

- Malpractice cases are often highly complex technically, involving issues such as surgical procedures, proper mediation or whether the patient's consent was properly obtained before an operation, appropriate operating procedures, or medical judgement and risk assessment by both the doctor and patient.

As a result of these considerations, some observations may be made regarding mediating these cases.

Timing of the Mediation

- A mediation that occurs before the injury is stable and the information about responsibility is sufficiently developed will not achieve agreement. Unless the doctor and/or hospital, through their insurer, is persuaded that there is real and substantial exposure to liability, the mediation will not succeed.

- Except in the most obvious cases of liability, the claimant will have to produce an expert opinion that the care was below the required standard. The opinion will have to be persuasive because there will usually be a similar expert report supporting the caregiver. The claimant's case must be sufficiently developed to disclose to the health professional's insurer or a significant risk of losing at trial in order to get them to the table in a meaningful way.

- The rules of procedure governing court process currently do not require the disclosure of the expert opinion relied upon by the doctor to support his contention that the caregiver was at or above the acceptable standard until ten days before trial. This is a significant barrier to early resolution of these cases unless the rule is waived or changed.

- The claimant's lawyer is reluctant to disclose or even obtain their expert's opinion until the health-care professional or hospital staff has been cross-examined under oath at discovery and their version of the facts is committed to transcript. The transcript is then turned over to their "expert" for comment and the claimant's opinion is produced.

- Similarly, the doctor's lawyer is unwilling to obtain an opinion until the transcripts of the cross-examination of both the doctor and patient are in hand, which only occurs after discovery.

⬛

Malpractice disputes are very expensive. Many claimants do not have the resources to undertake them. Currently many claimants' lawyers proceed with these cases on the basis that they will be paid from the proceeds, if successful. This practice will become more widespread with the official recognition of contingency fees, a subject of intense debate currently. If contingency fees are allowed, there may be a tremendous growth in these cases.

Parties to these disputes should find a way to negotiate cooperatively, recognizing that it is in their interest, as well as society's, to resolve these cases as quickly and inexpensively as possible.

Appropriate Party

Anger and emotion are ever present in medical cases. While the injuring party/wrongdoer is generally unavailable in personal injury cases, the doctor, nurse, or other health-care provider is, and should attend the mediation to really give mediation a chance. Having the doctor or health-care provider present allows the injured party to express his emotions and allows the other to respond and explain empathically. This catharsis is usually critical to resolving these cases.

Complaints About Doctors and Other Health-Care Professionals

Physical injuries caused by negligence and complaints about professional misconduct such as sexual harassment are currently dealt with through mediation by many of the health-care organizations. The College of Physicians and Surgeons of Ontario has instituted a programme of mediation involving the patient, doctor, and a representative of the College.

Many other self-regulating health-care providers are contemplating following suit. Mediation provides a speedy, private, and relatively inexpensive way to resolve highly personal and sensitive disputes.

Case Study

A young woman was treated in a rural hospital for symptoms that were diagnosed as a digestive disorder. The symptoms persisted and her condition worsened to such an extent that she was rushed to hospital in Toronto. After a battery of tests were performed, she was diagnosed with a rare and extremely aggressive form of cancer, which proved fatal. The husband sued the family physician and rural hospital claiming that they were both negligent in failing to diagnose the cancer.

During the mediation it emerged that the doctor had gone away on a holiday shortly before the crisis that resulted in the emergency trip to Toronto. As well, the doctor's lawyer tabled a report from a respected expert to the effect that the rare form of cancer could and usually did run its course in a matter of a few short weeks.

The hospital made a plea to be "let out" of the litigation on the basis that the doctor was not employed by the hospital and therefore it could not be responsible for the doctor's acts even if she had been negligent, which they doubted. Furthermore, the hospital stated that they had done all in their power to save the woman.

The husband had not been able to obtain an opinion condemning the care of either the doctor or the hospital.

It became apparent during the mediation that the grief-stricken husband really wanted answers about his wife's untimely death and was extremely angry about the doctor's absence on holidays. The CMPA, on behalf of the doctor, made it clear that, based on their expert's opinion, they had a defensible case and would under no circumstances make any payment to settle the case.

Despite this, the matter was settled, for three important reasons. The CMPA on behalf of the doctor agreed to let the husband meet with their expert so that he could get the answers he needed. Second, the doctor provided a sincere apology for not having been present and for creating the impression of insensitivity. Lastly, the husband had limited resources and could ill-afford the only other alternative open to him—to continue what would have been a tremendously expensive lawsuit which had the potential to bankrupt him if it failed.

While I cite this case as an example of a successful medical malpractice mediation, all too many fail. They fail because the claimant does not have the unequivocal opinion of an expert supporting the claim of medical negligence needed to persuade the medical professional and/or hospital of their exposure to liability. They fail because the policy of the defendants appears to be to settle only those cases where liability is patently obvious based on their concern that if they were to adopt a more conciliatory approach, the floodgates of claims would open and they would be deluged with claims, as has been the experience in some American jurisdictions.

GOVERNMENT DISPUTES

In Canada there are, depending on where you live, at least three levels of government: federal, provincial, and municipal. It is not surprising that corporations and individuals often find themselves in conflict with government. Various governmental tribunals, boards, and commissions have been established to deal with a myriad of laws, by-laws, rules, and regulations, and many have a specific dispute resolution procedure. These disputes may be extremely complex involving not only government agencies but many other affected parties.

Fortunately, both the federal government and many provincial governments, including Ontario, have recognized the need to streamline and simplify the regulatory jungle. They actively promote mediation whenever possible. In Ontario, mediation is a required first step in the dispute resolution processes of the following:

- the Ontario Municipal Board;
- the Workers' Compensation Board;
- the Environmental Assessment Board;
- the Commercial Licensing Board.

The office of the Ontario Ombudsman has recently endorsed the use of mediation whenever possible. It would be reasonable to expect that as a result of the ongoing restructuring of administrative tribunals in Ontario, many more agencies, boards, and commissions will adopt a mandatory mediation policy to allow the people to have greater input into how their disputes are resolved.

Provincial governments across Canada are studying the use of mediation. If you are involved in a dispute with government at any level or are in conflict with a government agency, board, or commission, you should inquire whether mediation of your dispute is an option.

Governments are becoming increasingly mindful of the cost savings achieved by allowing, indeed encouraging, parties in conflict to settle their own disputes provided the interests of the government and public are protected. Mediation is ideally suited to achieving these goals.

Case Study

A mediator/writer who has requested anonymity, recently, had an interesting interaction with government. It involved an application for a pond permit required by a law protecting an environmentally sensitive escarpment area. This application was submitted in the fall anticipating the construction could be started in spring with early summer completion. Apparently, the local municipality was notified and he was advised that the municipality had objected to the application and a hearing would be necessary. Another authority who had also received notice mused that because a dam was involved, perhaps an engineering study would be required.

He asked the pond builder to show him the dam on the plan. The builder pointed to an elevated bank. He then asked for a copy of the municipality's objection and received a copy of a three-line letter to the effect that the municipality was concerned due to the "proliferation of ponds in the area and their possible effect on the water table." He attempted to find out more about this without any luck. On the advice of the pond contractor, he withdrew the first application. The second application had a reduced bank which overcame one objection but the municipality repeated its objection. A hearing before a three-person board took place in due course. The municipality did not see fit to attend. The evidence of "proliferation" was never put forward; however, the evidence of the pond builder was that the area of the pond contained at least seven springs and the water table was not in jeopardy in the least.

One might say all is well that ends well. However, from the citizen's perspective, the municipality acted in a clumsy, oafish fashion. The pond was delayed by two years and several hundred dollars were wasted in obtaining reports and opinions in a very simple matter. This could all have been avoided had a meeting been held early between the municipality, the planner for the board, the conservation authority, and the pond builder.

There are countless pieces of legislation out there, hundreds of agencies, boards, and commissions with very formal, rigid, and expensive processes designed to adjudicate disputes between citizens and government regulators. Very few people have the time, money, patience, or expertise to cope with this often oppressive machinery of government. Whether it be workers' compensation, property tax reassessments, or immigration matters, to name but a few of the day-to-day encounters citizens have with government, one would think that designing an early mediation event into the process, requiring the parties to negotiate, would be a sensible course to follow before requiring the citizen to appear, cap in hand, for relief before boards and tribunals which cost umpteen thousands of dollars to operate daily.

NEIGHBOURHOOD AND COMMUNITY DISPUTES

Community disputes can arise over just about anything: a fence, a garage, a wall, an eyesore, noise pollution, a building project, children's behaviour, racial tensions, teenage pranks, a renovation, weeds, pets, harassment of one sort or another, parking, or a cultural confrontation. Mediation has proven highly effective at not only resolving the particular incident but preventing, or lessening, future incidents. Mediation training has proven effective in giving communities conflict resolution skills that are reusable time and time again. Rather than calling in someone unfamiliar with the local terrain, having trusted members of the community trained in dispute resolution would benefit communities greatly. Mediation can be the dispute resolution gift that keeps on giving.

Community activism is on the rise, driven perhaps by government cutbacks and the realization that these days the squeaky wheel gets the grease. People want their problems solved locally with solutions that they perceive will address their concerns, not by some bureaucrat miles, or perhaps light years, away from their reality.

Much has been written and said about why mediation works in neighbourhood and community disputes. It seems self-evident that if parties are empowered to design a solution that works for them, without having it imposed, the result will tend to endure and be replicated by example.

Other forms of community mediation include programmes designed to teach our children conflict resolution skills in school. Sometimes called Peer Mediation, students are taught to mediate disputes in the school yard and classroom themselves. The idea of training children from an early age to negotiate peaceably to resolve conflict has considerable appeal.

Case Study (Hypothetical)

Racial and cultural intolerance and tensions seem, if anything, to be on the increase. Several injuries have occurred and lives have been lost in confrontations between police and protesting aboriginal peoples at Oka, Ipperwash, and Gustavsen Lake. Black youths have been killed, inquiries have been held, and criminal charges laid in an effort to find out what happened and to assign blame, if appropriate.

Despite these activities, the problems persist. Why? When inquiries and trials take place, what happens? The interested parties make submissions to the commission of inquiry or judge that are entirely self-serving and positional to vindicate themselves and escape blame. The defence points out all the reasons why the policeman is not guilty and the prosecution argues for a conviction.

During the inquiries various groups make submissions about racial prejudice within the police force. The police submissions refute these allegations focusing on crime rates and community problems. The commissioners, carefully chosen to provide a balanced view, write an earnest report which finds its way to dusty shelves containing many similar reports.

What if the parties decided to try a new approach where they would talk to one another privately away from the glare of publicity and media hype? What if they agreed not to speak to the press unless they did so jointly, refraining from trying to score points at each other's expense? What if the parties agreed to speak openly about their respective concerns, needs, and fears so that each side would have a better appreciation for the pushes and pulls that create each side's reality and solitude?

The police might explain that their culture is a highly militaristic one based on authority, obeying orders, and following rules unquestionably. Every complaint made against them is investigated and if their behaviour is blameworthy, it goes on their record, greatly affecting their careers and prospects for advancement. To apologize is tantamount to admitting guilt, for that matter, agreeing to mediate or negotiate might be taken by some to be a sign of weakness and be held against them. Or, they might be sued civilly for damages for using more force than was necessary and their insurers might deny coverage under their insurance policy if they made any damaging admissions. They might say that patrolling high crimes areas is very stressful and that several colleagues have been killed in the line of duty. Fear is their constant companion, fear of bodily harm, on the one hand, and fear of recriminations and public humiliation if they make a mistake, on the other.

The black or aboriginal community might speak of the grinding poverty and lack of self-esteem that accompanies having to accept government assistance. In the case of aboriginals, they could discuss what lack of self-determination has meant for them. They might speak of their concerns for their children who are jammed into inferior schools and exposed early to drugs and violence. They might express concern about the apparent insensitivity and racial bias they perceive exists in the police force and the apparent failure to actively recruit minorities and use them for community policing in their own community.

Each side would have an opportunity to present or request objective data in support of these statements so that each would understand that the statements were fairly made and not simply based on rhetoric. Having tested and probed each other's points of view to better understand them they might set to work discussing options that may address some, if not all, of their concerns. It would be unrealistic to suggest that problems that have existed for years could be resolved overnight. However, certain concrete measures might be agreed to remove the systemic hurdle that prevents the police from having a meaningful dialogue about improving racial relations or healing wounds resulting from police action. Recommendations might be agreed on for recruiting and community policing. An agreement might be reached to create a safe forum protected by a confidentiality agreement to continue the dialogue away from the media and the posturing that usually accompanies it.

They will have had an opportunity to educate one another about each other's facts of life in a process that doesn't deal in blame or who is right or wrong. They have nowhere to run, nowhere to hide. With willpower and the necessary authority, solutions that go a long way toward addressing their respective concerns may well be possible, provided they accept the challenge.

CONCLUSION

Mediation used wisely, well, and early has the potential to revolution-ize or transform the way we deal with one another in the business world and in our personal lives. Used poorly, mediation may deteriorate into yet another arcane and misunderstood tool of justice, joining the many other attempts at streamlining the justice system—on the scrap heap of failure.

The beauty of mediation is its simplicity, flexibility, and ability to deliv-er positive results. Much of the stress of day-to-day life arguably results from frustration at our inability to resolve conflicts quickly and humanely. How many times have we shrugged our shoulders and conceded defeat or failed to engage in any process to deal with disputes on a personal level and in busi-ness. The common refrain, "It's just not worth pursuing," is heard too often these days. Every time we opt out of resolving a dispute because the justice system, government, or society is unable to provide a straightforward and inexpensive process that has a good chance of producing a satisfying out-come, we all become a little poorer. Feelings of powerlessness, frustration, anger, and stress are the results, rather than harmony and reconciliation.

Mediation provides an alternative to simply stifling our disputes or allowing them to gather dust unresolved in our "to-do" files or the backs of our minds.

Essential to making the most of mediation is understanding that the process belongs to the people—not the mediators, lawyers, academics, trainers, or writers. Stripped down, mediation is simply a negotiation between parties with a difference of opinion. Only the most basic understanding of negotiation is required for you to conduct yourself with distinction in mediation.

This book argues that "assisted" negotiation has an excellent chance of resolving disputes in ways that provide a high degree of satisfaction, both with the process and most importantly with the result. This is because the mediation process interjects a neutral, with no stake in the outcome, to guide the course of the negotiation around and over the shoals and barriers when they threaten to swamp the boat. We like to think of ourselves as self-reliant, competent, rugged individualists. If our initial negotiations fail, our competitive instincts find litigation appealing at first blush, the decision usually taken out of frustration and anger. Formerly litigation or inaction were the only options available to us. Now a third and very viable choice exists.

We don't hesitate to call in a plumber, electrician, or heart surgeon if we are having trouble in these areas. Why not try a mediator if we're having trouble resolving a dispute? There is absolutely no magic to what mediators and mediations do. Because the process and mediator are neutral and expert at helping the parties to understand both their own and their opponents' underlying interests, as well as skilled at overcoming the numerous barriers that keep them apart, they are able to make the way to agreement clear.

It isn't a sign of weakness to propose mediation, rather it is an indication of strength. To do so requires: confidence in the process, yourself, and your team's ability to find an appropriate way of resolving the dispute rather than abdicating the responsibility to someone else; courage in your convictions that automatically flows from a realistic and careful analysis of your essential interests, and those of your opponent, thereby enabling you to express them clearly and compellingly; humility in acknowledging that the chances of success without assistance are as slim as taking a couple of aspirins when a heart valve or arteries require the attention of a surgeon. Disputes that have reached or are well along the litigation highway require more than a placebo. They have acquired momentum which left unchecked becomes irreversible. Lastly, the energy and commitment to make the process meaningful by selecting the right mediator to design it, the appropriate players (such as your lawyer and others) to enhance and complete your preparation and participation, and adopting an open, flexible attitude to full engagement with your opponent to achieve a lasting and workable agreement.

All of this is well worth the effort. The payoff is instantaneous and substantial. Staying at the wheel rather than handing it over to others and staying in control of your personal or corporate destiny is its own reward. It is hoped that the insights, case studies, and glimpses behind the scenes contained in these pages will assist you in realizing the full potential of this amazing process.

APPENDIX A

GLOSSARY OF DISPUTE RESOLUTION TERMS

Accommodation A conflict resolution style which seeks to recognize the legitimacy of the opponents' needs and concerns.

ADR Alternate Dispute Resolution or Appropriate Dispute Resolution— terms used to describe non-traditional processes involving forms of negotiation or adjudication used to resolve disputes peacefully. Examples include mediation, arbitration, conciliation, negotiation, early neutral evaluation, fact finding and mini-trial.

Adjudication Traditional top-down dispute resolution where a decision is delivered by a designated "adjudicator" such as a judge, arbitrator or official who chooses between often extreme alternatives that favour only one of the disputants.

Advisory Opinion See also Pretrial. A non-binding opinion delivered by a neutral third party such as a judge or ex-judge after a brief examination of the positions put forward by the disputants or their counsel.

Agreement to Mediate (Arbitrate) An agreement entered into between the disputants and the mediator or arbitrator which establishes the relationship between them and sets out the way the parties will conduct themselves during the process, the nature of the dispute, ground rules relating to confidentiality, disclosure, privacy and other important terms that will govern the parties such as authority, fees, timing and location.

Arbitration A process designed by the parties and presided over by a neutral third party or a panel of experts headed by a chairperson. That person hears the arguments, the evidence advanced by the parties and their experts and delivers either a binding or non-binding award which favours one of the disputants over the other(s).

Arbitrator A neutral third party selected by the disputants, usually for his/her expertise in a particular field such as labour relations or commercial construction.

Authority One of two vital prerequisites to a successful mediation. Full authority means sufficient authority to conclude an agreement to resolve all outstanding issues on a reasonable basis, which implies flexibility and creativity as well as the ability to bind legally. Limited authority is authority restricted by conditions or financial limits or which must be ratified by a higher authority such as a board of directors, senior claims manager or municipal council. Such limits should be disclosed at the start of the negotiation or mediation.

Avoidance A conflict resolution style that seeks to retreat, minimize or appease rather than confront the source of disagreement.

Award The decision of the arbitrator or arbitration panel, issued at the conclusion of an arbitration.

Body Language Non-verbal communication, voluntary or involuntary, which conveys additional information to an observant negotiator or mediator. This includes, for example, eye contact or lack of it.

Caucus Sometimes referred to as a private meeting where one party or team meet together privately to discuss the progress of a negotiation. In a mediation, the term describes a private and confidential meeting of one side with the mediator.

Closure Bringing the discussion of an issue or issues to a focused conclusion, resulting either in agreement or an agreement to disagree.

Coercion A conflict resolution style that employs threats, power and intimidation to influence the desired outcome. Strike action, war, public or private character assassination, media campaigns and sanctions are all examples of coercion. Coercion is the handmaiden of positional negotiation.

Collaboration A conflict resolution style which treats the dispute as a problem-solving exercise, including all parties' concerns, needs and aspirations in seeking common ground and a mutually acceptable outcome.

Co-Mediation Employing two or more mediators when circumstances warrant, for example, multiissue/multiparty negotiations such as environmental, cross-cultural or public policy disputes.

Competitive A conflict resolution style which seeks to maximize gains at the expense of the opponent.

Compromise A style of conflict resolution which seeks to trade or make concessions in the hope of obtaining what is required to achieve an acceptable outcome.

Conciliation A conciliator or neutral person is employed to shuttle messages between hostile disputants in an effort to reduce hostilities and create conditions for productive face-to-face negotiations. It is often erroneously confused with mediation where the mediator is much more proactive in designing and controlling the process. Conciliation is often imposed on the parties by government in an attempt to break deadlocked negotiations, as for example, in labour disputes.

Confidentiality An essential ingredient of mediation agreed to as a prerequisite by the parties in order to encourage open dialogue and full disclosure of information critical to achieving successful resolution.

Conflict Management Styles Accommodation, Avoidance, Compromise, Collaboration, Coercion and Competitive are some of the various styles of conflict management employed singly or in combination by disputants.

Costs May be "legal costs" incurred prosecuting or defending a claim in court. Sometimes referred to as "court costs" which are awarded to the winner and paid by the loser. "Transaction Costs" sometimes used by negotiators in analysing their walk-away position and that of their opponents. Transaction costs may include legal and court costs as well as opportunity, economic, psychological and organizational costs incurred by a party while engaged in a dispute.

Cross-Cultural Conflict A dispute involving different ethnic, gender or religious perspectives which must be understood and communicated sensitively and forthrightly in order to achieve a mutually satisfactory outcome.

Damages The amount of compensation awarded by a court to successful claimants or plaintiffs in an attempt to compensate them for their loss or put them back in the same position they were in before the event which prompted the lawsuit, for example, before the breach of contract, car accident or wrongful termination of employment.

Defendant The party named in a lawsuit by the plaintiff who must respond to the claim.

Discovery A litigation process used in a lawsuit to achieve disclosure of relevant information, both written and verbal, through the use of cross-examination. Each party's lawyer cross-examines the other party exhaustively under oath about all relevant aspects of the case. The questions and answers are recorded and the resulting transcript forms part of the court record and may be used by either party during the trial.

Early Neutral Evaluation A voluntary ADR process which involves the disputants and their lawyers appearing before a mutually respected neutral third party such as a judge, senior lawyer, expert, or court official at an early stage in the lawsuit. Each side presents arguments and receives a non-binding advisory opinion on the issues. This process is often sometimes used to good effect to break an impasse on difficult points during a mediation.

Facilitator A neutral individual who assists groups to achieve their stated objectives and to work productively and harmoniously. The term is often used erroneously for a mediator.

Fact Finding A dispute resolution process which employs a neutral to investigate facts in dispute and incorporate the results in a report which can be binding or merely informative.

Ground Rules Those terms and conditions which the parties agree will govern the conduct of the mediation, for example, "no interrupting a speaker."

Impasse A barrier to agreement which if not overcome during the mediation despite everyone's best efforts, will result in deadlock ending the mediation.

Intervention A point during mediation where the mediator literally steps in with a suggestion, a summary of progress, a question or statement designed to refocus, restate or reflect one party's point of view in an effort to move the process and agenda forward.

Judgement/Order A written or oral decision of a judge or court official favouring one litigant over another, and containing, for example, the amount of damages and costs to be awarded the winner and paid by the loser. Such judgements if not paid may be enforced by a court official (sheriff), seizing and selling assets of the loser.

Liability In civil litigation the equivalent of guilt in a criminal trial. To be found liable for damages in a breach-of-contract case means having judgement entered for the amount awarded.

Listening Actively A technique employed by skilful negotiators and mediators to maximize their understanding of the speaker's point of view. Active listening generally probes beneath the surface for underlying interests while demonstrating understanding and empathy towards the speaker. It demonstrates the meaning of the expression "listening is more than simply waiting for an opportunity to speak."

Litigation A dispute resolution process administered by the courts. A lawsuit is launched by the plaintiff or claimant against defendant(s) from whom the claimant seeking relief, usually compensation, for example, a breach of contract or a legally wrongful act or omission. Lawyers are generally employed by the disputants. The process includes exchanges of information called discoveries, often a pretrial or settlement meeting and ultimately a trial before a judge.

Note: In Ontario as of January 31, 1997, mediation became a compulsory step in this process. It started in Ottawa on February 1, 1997, in Toronto in the fall of 1997, and will be phased in throughout the province over the following four years.

Mediation Mediation is a dispute resolution process that employs a neutral, impartial third party to assist the disputing parties to negotiate a mutually satisfactory outcome or agreement. The mediator, with input from the parties and their lawyers, structures the negotiation to maximize the possibility of resolution by fostering direct communication between the parties and full disclosure of information in a businesslike environment.

Mediator One who literally comes between parties in conflict. Someone who has no stake in the dispute and is skilled and experienced at helping people find their own solutions for their problems.

Mediation–Arbitration A dispute resolution process in which the parties agree to begin as a mediation and if impasse occurs revert to an arbitration. While this process will invariably produce a result either because it is imposed or because the parties reach agreement, the process is skewed towards persuading the mediator of the merits of each disputant's case. (Sometimes called Med-Arb.)

Mini-Trial A dispute resolution process which employs a panel of knowledgeable individuals, typically one designated by each disputant, chaired by a neutral, who hear the arguments and evidence from each side. The process is designed by the parties and may include questioning of witnesses, especially experts, even questioning of counsel. The panel then delivers a decision which may be binding or advisory as may have been preagreed by the parties.

Negotiation The most widely known and used form of dispute resolution involving direct communication between the disputants with the objective of resolving the dispute. Negotiation theory has evolved to the point where various types of negotiation have been identified. *Interest-based or Win/Win Negotiation* is based on the objective merits and the underlying interests of each party's case. The approach is one of problem solving based on shared objective information. *Win/Lose Positional Negotiation* (sometimes called Principled Negotiation) assumes that there will be a winner and a loser. The negotiators see themselves as adversaries and resort to strategic behaviour calculated to achieve "success" at the other's expense. The prevailing climate is one of distrust. Information tends to be shared selectively in order to manipulate and get the better of the deal. (Sometimes called Distributive Negotiation.)

Open Questions Questions posed by a skilled negotiator or mediator which probe and attempt to elicit more than a yes or no answer. Used to probe positions and obtain information revealing underlying interests.

Ombudsman An official designated by large institutions such as governments, universities and more recently banks to investigate complaints and prepare reports (See Fact Finding), recommending ways and means of resolving the complaint. The idea originated in Sweden but was quickly adopted by Canada which is now considered a world leader in developing and finding new applications for this very versatile concept.

Partnering A conflict anticipation and containment process used principally in the construction industry. A facilitator gets all interested parties together prior to the start of the project, in a team-building exercise, designed to create lasting relationships and a code of conduct to identify and resolve disputes as they arise.

Plaintiff The party asserting a claim in a lawsuit, sometimes referred to as claimant.

Pretrial Sometimes called a settlement meeting in which the lawyers appear before a judge and briefly put forward their respective positions. The judge provides a non-binding advisory opinion. Used in litigation as a last-ditch effort to settle a case before trial. Thought by many to be too little, too late.

Private Judging or Rent-A-Judge Refers to a dispute resolution process often confused with mediation. An ex-judge or senior lawyer, after hearing the arguments and evidence, provides a non-binding decision, as in Early Neutral Evaluation; the matter may proceed more formally by agreement between the parties as an arbitration.

APPENDIX B

The following agreement is intended as a guide or "typical" agreement but is not one to be used slavishly. The agreement to mediate discussion in Chapter 3, as well as the checklist provided, should be your guide.

AGREEMENT TO MEDIATE

Between

_____

and

_____

(the Parties)

and

_____

(the Mediator)

1. Purpose of the Mediation. Mediation is assisted negotiation during which the parties work together in an effort to achieve a fair and mutually agreeable settlement of their dispute. In entering into this agreement, the parties and their counsel affirm their intention to work cooperatively and constructively towards attaining this objective.

2. Description of Dispute. The parties agree to the mediation process in order to resolve a dispute between them, the essential facts of which are as follows:

_____

_____

_____

_____

_____

_____

_____

_____

_____

3. Disclosure. Cooperation and good faith are essential to the mediation process. The parties agree to disclose to each other all information which is relevant to the dispute.

4. Confidentiality. Mediation is a private process. The parties and mediator agree to keep all information exchanged in the mediation confidential. Statements made or information disclosed by a party will not be divulged outside the mediation or used in any subsequent legal proceedings unless all parties consent. This does not include any final settlement agreed to in writing and signed by the parties. The parties may agree in writing that this will also be confidential.

5. Mediator Cannot Be a Witness. In any subsequent legal proceedings between the parties, the mediator cannot be called as a witness.

6. Termination of Mediation. Since mediation is a voluntary form of negotiation, either party or the mediator may terminate the process at any time, for any reason.

7. Role of the Mediator. The mediator's role is to act as a neutral facilitator in the parties' negotiations. The mediator does not provide any legal advice, decide any issues between the parties, or make judgements relating to the merits of the parties' cases. While the mediator may meet privately with either party during the mediation, anything revealed to the mediator will not be disclosed to another party without consent. The mediator will also disclose any conflict of interest with either party prior to entering into this agreement.

8. Role of Counsel. If the parties retain counsel for the mediation, their role is to ensure that their clients' interests are satisfied, and that any settlement agreement is legal and enforceable. As such, the parties' counsel undertake to prepare their clients for the mediation process and to review this agreement with them, as well as to prepare any settlement agreement which may be reached.

9. Mediation Fee. The parties agree to share the costs of this mediation equally. These costs include:

(i) a Mediation Fee per party of $ for each   hour session or part thereof including preparation time;

(ii) all reasonable travel, hotel, telephone, fax, food or other administrative expenses incurred by the mediator in respect of the mediation;

(iii) an Administrative Fee for each party of $ which is payable at the time of signing this agreement and which is not refundable.

Mediation is a voluntary process, and thus either party may cancel the mediation at their discretion. However, if either party cancels less than   hours before the time scheduled for a mediation session, that party must pay a cancellation fee of $. This will be in addition to the Administrative Fee.

10. Third Parties. The mediator may meet with third parties who might have a bearing on this dispute if this would be of benefit to the mediation process. This will be done only with the consent of all the parties.

11. Time and Place. The mediation session will take place on the   day of   , 19   , at   o'clock. The mediation will be held at

Subsequent sessions, if they are necessary, will be held at times agreeable to the parties and the mediator, and will be subject to the provisions of this agreement.

12. Indemnity. The parties agree that they will indemnify and save harmless the mediator from all costs or claims which they may now have, or might have in the future, respecting or arising from this mediation.

13. Altering the Agreement. This agreement may not be altered other than in writing and with the written consent of all the parties and the mediator.

I have read, understand, and agree to the provisions of this agreement.

_____   _____

Signature of party   Date

_____   _____

Counsel   Date

_____   _____

Signature of party   Date

_____   _____

Counsel   Date

_____   _____

Signature of Mediator   Date

APPENDIX C

ARBITRATION AND MEDIATION INSTITUTE OF CANADA INC.

These codes of ethics are included for reference on the current state of thought governing mediator ethics.

The Arbitration and Mediation Institute of Canada's code is only subscribed to by its membership.

Code of Ethics

Application

This Code is applicable to all members of the Institute in their capacity as arbitrators and mediators generally and in their undertaking of an arbitration or mediation appointment specifically.

Code

1. A Member shall uphold and abide by the Rules of Conduct, regulations and other professional requirements adopted by the Institute.

2. A Member shall not carry on any activity or conduct which could reasonably be considered as conduct unbecoming a member of the Institute.

3. A Member shall uphold the integrity and fairness of the arbitration and mediation processes.

4. A Member shall ensure that the parties involved in an arbitration or mediation are fairly informed and have an adequate understanding of the procedural aspects of the process and of their obligations to pay for services rendered.

5. A Member shall satisfy himself/herself that he/she is qualified to undertake and complete an appointment in a professional manner.

6. A Member shall disclose any interest or relationship likely to affect impartiality or which might create an appearance of partiality or bias.

7. A Member, in communicating with the parties, shall avoid impropriety or the appearance of impropriety.

8. A Member shall conduct all proceedings fairly and diligently, exhibiting independence and impartiality.

9. A Member shall be faithful to the relationship of trust and confidentiality inherent in the office of arbitrator or mediator.

10. A Member shall conduct all proceedings related to the resolution of a dispute in accordance with applicable law.

MODEL STANDARDS OF CONDUCT FOR MEDIATORS

The Model Standards of Conduct for Mediators were prepared from 1992 through 1994 by a joint committee composed of two delegates from the American Arbitration Association, John D. Feerick, Chair, and David Botwinik, two from the American Bar Association, James Alfini and Nancy Rogers, and two from the Society of Professionals in Dispute Resolution, Susan Dearborn and Lemoine Pierce.

The Model Standards have been approved by the American Arbitration Association, the Litigation Section and the Dispute Resolution Section of the American Bar Association, and the Society of Professionals in Dispute Resolution.

Reporters: Bryant Garth and Kimberlee K. Kovach

Staff Project Director: Frederick E. Woods

The views set out in this publication have not been considered by the American Bar Association House of Delegates and do not constitute the policy of the American Bar Association.

Introductory Note

The initiative for these standards came from three professional groups: The American Arbitration Association, the American Bar Association, and the Society of Professionals in Dispute Resolution.

The purpose of this initiative was to develop a set of standards to serve as a general framework for the practice of mediation. The effort is a step in the development of the field and a tool to assist practitioners in it—a beginning, not an end. The model standards are intended to apply to all types of mediation. It is recognized, however, that in some cases the application of these standards may be affected by laws or contractual agreements.

Preface

The model standards of conduct for mediators are intended to perform three major functions: to serve as a guide for the conduct of mediators; to inform the mediating parties; and to promote public confidence in mediation as a process for resolving disputes. The standards draw on existing codes of conduct for mediators and take into account issues and problems that have surfaced in mediation practice. They are offered in the hope that they will serve an educational function and provide assistance to individuals, organizations and institutions involved in mediation.

I. Self-Determination: A Mediator Shall Recognize that Mediation Is Based on the Principle of Self-Determination By the Parties.

Self-determination is the fundamental principle of mediation. It requires that the mediation process rely upon the ability of the parties to reach a voluntary, uncoerced agreement. Any party may withdraw from mediation at any time.

Comments

The mediator may provide information about the process, raise issues and help parties explore options. The primary role of the mediator is to facilitate a voluntary resolution of a dispute. Parties shall be given the opportunity to consider all proposed options.

A mediator cannot personally ensure that each party has made a fully informed choice to reach a particular agreement, but it is a good practice for the mediator to make the parties aware of the importance of consulting other professionals, where appropriate, to help them make informed decisions.

II. Impartiality: A Mediator shall Conduct the Mediation in an Impartial Manner.

The concept of mediator impartiality is central to the mediation process. A mediator shall mediate only those matters in which she or he can remain impartial and even-handed. If at any time the mediator is unable to conduct the process in an impartial manner, the mediator is obligated to withdraw.

Comments:

A mediator shall avoid conduct that gives the appearance of partiality towards one of the parties. The quality of the mediation process is enhanced when the parties have confidence in the impartiality of the mediator.

When mediators are appointed by a court or institution, the appointing agency shall make reasonable efforts to ensure that mediators serve impartially.

A mediator should guard against partiality or prejudice based on the parties' personal characteristics, backgrounds or performances at the mediation.

III. Conflicts of Interest: A mediator shall disclose all actual and potential conflicts of interest reasonably known to the mediator. After disclosure, the mediator shall decline to mediate unless all parties choose to retain the mediator. The need to protect against conflicts of interest also governs conduct that occurs during and after the mediation.

A conflict of interest is a dealing or relationship that might create an impression of possible bias. The basic approach to questions of conflict of interest is consistent with the concept of self-determination. The mediator has a responsibility to disclose all actual and potential conflicts that are reasonably known to the mediator and could reasonably be seen as raising a question about impartiality. If all parties agree to mediate after being informed of conflicts, the mediator may proceed with the mediation. If, however, the conflict of interest casts serious doubt on the integrity of the process, the mediator shall decline to proceed.

A mediator must avoid the appearance of conflict of interest both during and after the mediation. Without the consent of all parties, a mediator shall not subsequently establish a professional relationship with one of the parties in a related matter, or in an unrelated matter under circumstances which would raise legitimate questions about the integrity of the mediation process.

Comments:

A mediator shall avoid conflicts of interest in recommending the services of other professionals. A mediator may make reference to professional referral services or associations which maintain rosters of qualified professionals.

Potential conflicts of interest may arise between administrators of mediation programmes and mediators and there may be strong pressures on the mediator to settle a particular case or cases. The mediator's commitment must be to the parties and the process. Pressure from outside of the mediation process should never influence the mediator to coerce parties to settle.

IV. Competence: A mediator shall mediate only when the mediator has the necessary qualifications to satisfy the reasonable expectations of the parties.

Any person may be selected as a mediator, provided that the parties are satisfied with the mediator's qualifications. Training and experience in mediation, however, are often necessary for effective mediation. A person who offers herself or himself as available to serve as a mediator gives parties and the public the expectation that she or he has the competency to mediate effectively. In court-connected or other forms of mandated mediation, it is essential that mediators assigned to the parties have the requisite training and experience.

Comments:

Mediators should have information available for the parties regarding their relevant training, education and experience.

The requirements for appearing on the list of mediators must be made public and available to interested persons.

When mediators are appointed by a court or institution, the appointing agency shall make reasonable efforts to ensure that each mediator is qualified for the particular mediation.

V. Confidentiality: A mediator shall maintain the reasonable expectations of the parties with regard to confidentiality.

The reasonable expectations of the parties with regard to confidentiality shall be met by the mediator. The parties' expectations of confidentiality depend on the circumstances of the mediation and any agreements they may make. The mediator shall not disclose any matter that a party expects to be confidential unless given permission by all parties or unless required by law or other public policy.

Comments:

The parties may make their own rules with respect to confidentiality, or other accepted practice of an individual mediator or institution may dictate a particular set of expectations. Since the parties' expectations regarding confidentiality are important, the mediator should discuss these expectations with the parties.

If the mediator holds private sessions with a party, the nature of these sessions with regard to confidentiality should be discussed prior to undertaking such sessions.

In order to protect the integrity of the mediation, a mediator should avoid communicating information about how the parties acted in the mediation process, the merits of the case or settlement offers. The mediator may report, if required, whether parties appeared at a scheduled mediation.

Where the parties have agreed that all or a portion of the information disclosed during a mediation is confidential, the parties' agreement should be respected by the mediator.

Confidentiality should not be construed to limit or prohibit the effective monitoring, research or evaluation of mediation programmes by responsible persons. Under appropriate circumstances, researchers may be permitted to obtain access to the statistical data and, with the permission of the parties, to individual case files, observations of live mediations and interviews with participants.

VI. Quality of the Process: A mediator shall conduct the mediation fairly, diligently, and in a manner consistent with the principle of self-determination by the parties.

A mediator shall work to ensure a quality process and to encourage mutual respect among the parties. A quality process requires a commitment by the mediator to diligence and procedural fairness. There should be adequate opportunity for each party in the mediation to participate in the discussions. The parties decide when and under what conditions they will reach an agreement or terminate a mediation.

Comments:

A mediator may agree to mediate only when he or she is prepared to commit the attention essential to an effective mediation.

Mediators should only accept cases when they can satisfy the reasonable expectations of the parties concerning the timing of the process. A mediator should not allow a mediation to be unduly delayed by the parties or their representatives.

The presence or absence of persons at a mediation depends on the agreement of the parties and the mediator. The parties and mediator may agree that others may be excluded from particular sessions or from the entire mediation process.

The primary purpose of a mediator is to facilitate the parties' voluntary agreement. This role differs substantially from other professional-client relationships. Mixing the role of a mediator and the role of a professional advising a client is problematic, and mediators must strive to distinguish between the roles. A mediator should, therefore, refrain from providing professional advice. Where appropriate, a mediator should recommend that parties seek outside professional advice, or consider resolving their dispute through arbitration, counseling, neutral evaluation or other processes. A mediator who undertakes, at the request of the parties, an additional dispute resolution role, in the same matter assumes increased responsibilities and obligations that may be governed by the standards of other processes.

A mediator shall withdraw from a mediation when incapable of serving or when unable to remain impartial.

A mediator shall withdraw from a mediation or postpone a session if the mediation is being used to further illegal conduct, or if a party is unable to participate due to drug, alcohol, or other physical or mental incapacity.

Mediators should not permit their behaviour in the mediation process to be guided by a desire for a high settlement rate.

VII. Advertising and Solicitation: A mediator shall be truthful in advertising and solicitation for mediation

Advertising or any other communication with the public, concerning services offered or regarding the education, training and expertise of the mediator, shall be truthful. Mediators shall refrain from promises and guarantees of results.

Comments:

It is imperative that communication with the public educate and instil confidence in the process.

In an advertisement or other communication to the public, a mediator may make reference to meeting state, national or private organization qualifications only if the entity referred to has a procedure for qualifying mediators and the mediator has been duly granted the requisite status.

VIII. Fees: A mediator shall fully disclose and explain the basis of compensation, fees, and charges to the parties.

The parties should be provided sufficient information about fees at the outset of a mediation to determine if they wish to retain the services of a mediator. If a mediator charges fees, the fees shall be reasonable, considering
among other things, the mediation service, the type and complexity of the
matter, the expertise of the mediator, the time required and the rates customary in the community. The better practice in reaching an understanding
about fees is to set down the arrangements in a written agreement.

Comments:

A mediator who withdraws from a mediation should return any unearned fee
to the parties.
     A mediator should not enter into a fee agreement which is contingent
upon the result of the mediation or amount of the settlement.
     Co-mediators who share a fee should hold to standards of reasonable-
ness in determining the allocation of fees.
     A mediator should not accept a fee for referral of a matter to another
mediator or to any other person.

IX. Obligations to the Mediation Process: Mediators have a duty to improve the practice of mediation.

Comments:

Mediators are regarded as knowledgeable in the process of mediation. They
have an obligation to use their knowledge to help educate the public about
mediation; to make mediation accessible to those who would like to use it;
to correct abuses; and to improve their professional skills and abilities.

LIST OF
REFERENCES

BOOKS AND MANUALS

Arrow, K., ed. *Barriers to Conflict Resolution.* New York: Norton, 1995.

Brown, Henry J. *ADR Principles and Practice.* London: Sweet & Maxwell, 1993.

Bush, Robert A. Baruch & Joseph P. Folger. *The Promise of Mediation: Responding to Conflict Through Empowerment and Recognition.* San Francisco: Jossey-Bass, 1994.

Canadian Bar Association. *Alternative Dispute Resolution: A Canadian Perspective.* Ottawa: Canadian Bar Association, 1989.

Crosby, Doreen. *The Use of Mediation in Settling Injury Claims: A Cost/Benefit Analysis.* Insurance Corporation of British Columbia (Alternative Dispute Resolution), July 1995.

Folberg, Jay & Allison Taylor. *Mediation.* San Francisco: Jossey-Bass, 1984.

Hoffman, Ben. *Win-Win Competitiveness Made in Canada.* North York, Ont.: Captus Press, 1993.

Hoffman, Ben. *Conflict Power Persuasion: Negotiating Effectively.* North York, Ont.: Captus Press, 1990.

Mackenzie, Gavin. *Lawyers & Ethics: Professional Responsibility and Discipline.* Toronto: Carswell, 1993.

McLaren, Richard & John Sanderson. *Innovative Dispute Resolution: The Alternative.* Toronto: Carswell, 1994.

Moore, Christopher. *The Mediation Process: Practical Strategies for Resolving Conflict.* 2nd. ed. San Francisco: Jossey-Bass, 1996.

Murray, John. *Processes of Dispute Resolution: The Role of the Lawyer.* Westbury, New York: Foundation Press, 1996.

National Institute for Dispute Resolution. *Dispute Resolution in State Courts: Sample Task Force and Commission Reports, Resource Notebook I.* NIDR, Spring 1993.

Ordover, Abraham P. *Alternatives to Litigation: Mediation, Arbitration and the Art of Dispute Resolution.* Indianapolis: Notre Dame, National Institute for Trial Advocacy, 1993.

Potter, Beverley. *From Conflict to Cooperation: How to Mediate a Dispute.* Berkeley, Calif.: Ronin Publishers, 1996.

Schwarz, Roger M. *The Skilled Facilitator: Practical Wisdom For Developing Effective Groups.* San Francisco: Jossey-Bass, 1996.

Slaikeu, Karl. *When Push Comes to Shove: A Practical Guide to Mediating Disputes.* San Francisco: Jossey-Bass, 1996.

Ury, William. *Getting Past No: Negotiating With Difficult People.* New York: Bantam Books, 1991.

Various Authors, *Ontario Court of Justice: Ontario Civil Justice Review.* Toronto: Publications Ontario, March 1995.

JOURNAL ARTICLES

Atlas, Hon. Nancy F. "Mediation in Bankruptcy Cases—Part I." *The Practical Lawyer* 41 (September 1995): 39-58.

Atlas, Hon. Nancy F. "Mediation in Bankruptcy Cases—Part II." *The Practical Lawyer* 41 (October 1995): 63.

Berlin, Robert A. "Mediation From A to Z." *Dispute Resolution Journal* (March 1994): 31.

Bowal, Peter. "The New Ontario Judicial Alternative Dispute Resolution Model." *Alberta Law Review* 34 (October 1995): 205-14.

Brand, Norman. "Learning to Use the Mediation Process—A Guide for Lawyers." *Arbitration Journal* 47 (December 1992): 6-12.

Brett, Jeanne M., Zoe I. Barsness, & Stephen B. Goldberg. "The Effectiveness of Mediation: An Independent Analysis of Cases Handled by Four Major Service Providers." *Negotiation Journal* (July 1996): 259-69.

Carver, Todd B. & Albert A. Vondra. "Alternative Dispute Resolution: Why it Doesn't Work and Why it Does." *Harvard Business Review* (May-June 1994): 120-30.

Conrod, Monique. "Delay, Expense Common Roadblocks to Civil Justice." *The Lawyers Weekly* (March 15, 1996): 7.

Cravez, Glenn E. "Eight Mediation Myths: Comments From the No-So-Frozen North." *Trial* 32 (June 1996): 24-26.

Elliot, David C. "Med/Arb: Fraught With Danger or Ripe With Opportunity?" *Alberta Law Review* 34 (October 1995): 163-77.

Feinsod, Paul M. "Where is Mediation or Arbitration for You?" *The Practical Lawyer* 35 (July 1989): 19-28.

Ferris, Heather M.B. "An Overview of the New Bankruptcy and Insolvency Act." *The Advocate* 50 (November 1992): 861-69.

Goss, Joanne. "An Introduction to Alternative Dispute Resolution." *Alberta Law Review* 34 (October 1995): 1-33.

Iacono, Paul. "Fitting the Forum: Which ADR Process is Best Suited to Your Dispute?" *Independent Adjuster* (December 1995): 16-18.

Iacono, Paul. "The ADR Imperative." *Focus on Property and General Liability Insurance* 1: 87-88.

Krivis, Jeffrey. "Insurers and Lawyers Unified on Mediation" *Best's Review* (March 1995): 70-71.

Law Society of Upper Canada, Subcommittee on Dispute Resolution, "Report Summary (Dispute Resolution Subcommittee Report)." (February 1993).

Meyer, Judith. "Mediation Works...With the Least Damage Done to the Parties' Egos and Pocketbooks." *Dispute Resolution Journal* (April 1995): 44-47.

Meyer, Tammy J. "Learning the Art of Negotiation." *For the Defense* (January 1996): 20-27.

Mnookin, Robert H. "Why Negotiations Fail: An Exploration of Barriers to the Resolution of Conflict." *The Ohio State Journal on Dispute Resolution* 8 (1993): 235-49.

Ornstil, Michael G. "Nailing Down Mediation Agreements." *Trial* 32 (June 1996): 18-22.

Phillips, Layn R. "Questions for Proposed Mediators." Trial 32 (June 1996): 30.

Shorten, Lynda. "Legal Update—Insolvency." *Canadian Lawyer* (October 1993): 37-42.

Shusterman, Spencer. "Litigation Controlling the Cost." *Canadian Insurance* (May 1995): 10-12.

Skumanich, Nonna & Denise Lach. "When Mediation Won't Work." *Washington State Bar News* (April 1993): 19-24.

Spolter, Jerry. "Checklist for Successful Mediation." *Dispute Resolution Journal* (March 1994): 26-30.

Various Authors. "Special Focus Section—Alternative Dispute Resolution." *The Lawyers Weekly* (January 26): 13-21.

Weinstein, Jeffrey L. & Tailim Song. "Advocacy in Mediation." *Trial* (June 1996): 29-33.

INDEX

Acknowledgement of other position, 66
ADR, 163
ADR spectrum, 1, 2
ADR street, 29-32
Agreement, 113-121
  breaking, 120
  confidentiality, 117
  dispute resolution clause, 119
  durable, 116
  efficient, 115
  enforceable, 116
  fair, 116
  legal advice, 120
  mediator, use of, 118
  tips, 117-120
Agreement to mediate, 50, 51, 173-176
Ali, the camel driver, 44
All-party brainstorming, 60
Anger, 91-96
Apology, 66
Arbitration, 31
  commercial cases, 125
  mediation, contrasted, 47
  what is it, 44, 45

Arbitration and Mediation Institute
  of Canada, code of ethics, 177, 178
Authority, 53

Bankruptcy and insolvency matters, 146-149
Barriers to success
  anger, 91-96
  bad timing, 105, 106
  bottom lines, 96-98
  cultural barriers, 108
  deadlock (impasse), 111, 112
  difficult behaviour, 104, 105
  difficult people, 103, 104
  disclosure of information, 102, 103
  institutional barriers, 111
  lack of preparation, 98-102
  lack of resources, 110
  missing party, 107
  overemphasis on preparation, 108
  power imbalances, 109
  unrealistic expectations, 106, 107
Best-case scenario, 11, 12
Body language, 54
Bonanza syndrome, 43

Bottom-line negotiation, 4-10
Bottom lines, 96-98
Brainstorming, 60
Breaks, 58
Business concessions, 67

Checklists
  interview guide, 89, 90
  mediation process, 72, 73
  preparation, 101, 102
Closure, 113-115
Codes of ethics, 177-184
College of Physicians and Surgeons of
    Ontario, 152
Commercial cases, 124-126
Community disputes, 156-158
Conciliation, 2, 165
Confidentiality, 82, 83, 117
Construction cases, 46, 140-143
Construction liens, 141
Corporate politics, 111
Cost avoidance, 68
Cultural barriers, 108

Deadlock. See Impasse
Decision to mediate, 35
Deemed reinvestment principle, 52
Definitions, 163-169
Difficult behaviour, 104, 105
Difficult people, 103, 104
Directive mediation, 80, 81
Disability claims, 131, 132
Disclosure of information, 41, 43, 102,
    103
Discoveries, 39, 40
Dispute resolution clause, 119
Disputes, classes of. See Types of
    disputes
Distributive negotiation, 4-10
Divorce mediation, 132-135

Early neutral evaluation, 3, 30
Empathy quotient (EQ), 77
Employment disputes, 135-139
Estate disputes, 143-145
Estate planning, 143, 144

Ethics
  legal, 87, 88
  mediator, 82, 83, 177-184

Fact finding, 3, 30, 31
Family business disputes, 139
Family councils, 139
Family mediation, 132-135
Family Mediation Canada, 85
Final agreement. See Agreement
Flexibility, 37

Glossary, 163-169
Goals, 54
Good publicity, 68
Government disputes, 154, 155
Ground rules, 52, 53

Hasher, 81
Humour, 16

Impasse, 14-16, 70, 71, 111, 112, 121
Inappropriate behaviour, 104, 105
Institutional barriers, 111
Intelligence quotient (IQ), 77
Interest-based mediation, 81
Interest-based negotiation, 4, 11-13
Interrupting, 55
Introductions, 52

Jackpot mentality, 43

Law, 100
Lawyer
  advisory role prior to litigation, 38
  difficult behaviour, 104, 105
  ethics, 87, 88
  personal injury cases, 130
  role, 86, 87
  written opinion, 106
Liability insurance, 80
Listening, 55, 56
Litigation
  delay factor, 28
  discovery, 39, 40
  escalation points, 39, 40

example (case study), 26, 27
historical context, 28, 29
myth of, 96
pleadings, 39
steps, in process, 22-25
Litigation mindset, 16-18
Loss aversion, 17

Mandatory court-connected
    mediation, 76, 77, 85
Mediation
  advantages, 32-35
  arbitration, contrasted, 47
  authority, 53
  barriers to success. *See* Barriers to
    success
  breaks, 58, 59
  checklist, 72, 73
  clarification/amplification, 57, 58
  closure, 113-115
  convening stage, 50-52
  court-connect programmes, 76, 77,
    85
  duration, 52
  elements of successful, 36-38
  general points, 32, 33
  generating options, 62
  getting other side to come to table,
    35, 36
  goals, 54
  ground rules, 52, 53
  impasse, 14-16, 70, 71, 111, 112, 121
  integrity of process, 83
  intention to negotiate in good faith,
    53
  introductions, 52, 53
  location, 51
  non-monetary elements of
    resolution. *See* Non-monetary
    elements of resolution
  opening statements, 55-57
  participation of parties, 55
  preparation, 98-102, 137
  private meetings, 58-60
  problem solving, 61
  reconvening, 60, 64

  role at table, 101
  testing alternatives, 62-64
  when to avoid, 42-44
  when to mediate, 38-42, 105, 106
  who should attend, 99, 107
Mediation/arbitration (Med-arb), 45,
    46
Mediation brief, 100
Mediation service providers, 84
Mediator
  bankruptcy cases, and, 147
  confidentiality, and, 82, 83
  conflict of interest, 82
  ethics, 82, 83, 177-184
  experience/training, 78
  facilitative vs. evaluative, 81
  final agreement, and, 118
  how to choose, 83-85, 89
  impartiality, 82
  knowledge of legal/technical issues,
    79
  liability insurance, 80
  overemphasis on settlement, 108
  personal history, 78
  qualities, 77
  role, 77, 82
  style, 80, 81
Mediator associations, 84, 85
Medical malpractice claims, 150-154
Mini-trial, 30
Model Standards of Conduct for
    Mediators, 178-184
Multiparty/multiissue disputes, 149, 150

Negotiation, 1-20
  creating value, 64, 65
  humour, 16
  impasse, 14-16
  interest-based (win/win), 4, 11-13
  positional (win/lose), 4-10
  power, 18, 19
  reactive devaluation, 13, 14
  style, 4, 13
  tips, 19, 20
Neighbourhood disputes, 156-158
Network for Conflict Resolution, 85

Non-monetary elements of
    resolution, 64, 65
  apology, 66
  avoiding bad precedent, 64
  avoiding bad publicity, 67, 68
  business concessions, 67
  cost avoidance, 68
  good publicity, 68
  money now vs. money later, 66
  risk aversion (certainty), 67
  stress avoidance, 67
  vindication/saving face, 65, 66
Note-taking, 56
Nothing-to-lose scenario, 44

Ombudsman, 154, 168
"On principle," 7
Opening statements, 55-57
Opponent's ability to pay, 110
Overvaluation, 17

Partnering, 141
Personal injury cases, 127-130
Positional negotiation, 4-10
Power imbalances, 18, 19, 109
Preparation, 98-102, 137
Private judging, 31, 169
Private meetings, 58-60

Reactive devaluation, 13, 14
Reference books, 185-188
Referral service, 85
Rent-a-Judge, 31, 169
Rights-based mediation, 31, 32, 80
Risk aversion, 17, 67
Role at table, 101

Saving face, 65, 66
Settlement remorse, 115. See also
    Agreement

Single-text agreement, 114
Statement of Claim, 39
Statement of Defence, 39
Stress avoidance, 67

Take-it-or-leave-it approach, 96
Third party, 60, 61
Tone of voice, 54
Trasher, 81
Types of disputes, 123-158
  bankruptcy and insolvency, 146-149
  commercial cases, 124-126
  construction cases, 140-143
  disability claims, 131, 132
  divorce/family mediation, 132-135
  employment disputes, 135-139
  family business disputes, 139
  government disputes, 154, 155
  medical malpractice claims, 150-154
  multiparty/multiissue disputes, 149,
    150
  neighbourhood/community
    disputes, 156-158
  personal injury cases, 127-130
  wrongful dismissal cases, 135-139

Unacceptable behaviour, 104, 105
Undervaluation, 17
Unrealistic expectations, 106, 107

Vindication, 65, 66

Walk-away position, 11, 12
Whack-um game, 14
Will, 144
Win/lose negotiation, 4-10
Win/win negotiation, 4, 11-13
Wrongful dismissal cases, 135-139

Zero-sum game, 8

THE AUTHOR

Norman A. Ross is a lawyer and mediator and practised law for over 22 years as a partner with a major international law firm. For the past three years, he has been one of two full-time mediators with the Alternative Dispute Resolution Centre in Toronto, a project sponsored by the Ontario Court of Justice and the Ministry of the Attorney-General. Daily during this period he mediated cases involving the entire scope of civil litigation lawsuits including insurance, estates, wrongful dismisal, construction and commercial disputes.

In 1995, Norman was the first to graduate as a specialist in Alternative Dispute Resolution from the Canadian International Institute of Applied Negotiation. He has conducted training in mediation, negotiation, and conflict resolution in both the private and public sectors. His work on mediation has been published by the Law Society of Upper Canada's *Gazette*, the Insurance Bureau of Canada, and the ADR Centre's *Release*.

He now practices as a private mediator and conflict resolution consultant based in Toronto, Ontario.

If you have any comments, opinions or general inquiries about conflict resolution programs or mediation services, or are interested in having the author conduct seminars or workshops for your group or association, please contact him through one of the methods below.

By fax:	416-544-0631
By telephone:	416-544-0633
By mail:	c.o. The Centre for Mediation 2300 Yonge Street, Suite 709 Toronto, Ontario M4P 1E4